# Daniel Unsealed

# Daniel Unsealed

## Breaking Open Understanding of Daniel's Prophecies

*A Collection of Original Articles
On End Times Theology*

Nelson Walters

With

Bob Brown

# Copyright 2019 by Nelson Walters

Unless otherwise noted, all Scripture quotations are taken from the New American Standard Bible® marked *NASB*, Copyright 1960, 1962, 1963, 1968, 1971, 1972, 1973, 1975, 1977, 1995 by The Lockman Foundation. Used by permission.

Scripture quotations marked "LXX" are from the Septuagint: Translation by Sir Lancelot C. L. Brenton, 1851, Public Domain.

All rights reserved solely by the author. No part of this book may be reproduced, stored in a retrieval system, or transmitted, in any form or by any means, electronic, mechanical, photocopying, recording, or otherwise, without the prior written permission of the author.

Because of the dynamic nature of the Internet, any web addresses or links contained in this book may have changed since publication and may no longer be valid.

*As always, special thanks to our good friend Joseph Lenard for his assistance in editing this book.*

**Ready For Jesus Publications (Wilmington, NC, 2018)**

**ISBN - 9781072946847**

# Contents

Article One .................................................................. 1
   What Are the Implications If Daniel Was Sealed?

Article Two ................................................................. 15
   Will the Fourth Kingdom Be Rome or the Islamic Caliphate?

Article Three ............................................................... 29
   The Beast from the Sea in Daniel 7

Article Four ................................................................ 53
   Where Will the Little Horn Come From?

Article Five ................................................................ 69
   The Four Beasts Are the Four Horns

Article Six ................................................................. 85
   The Rise of the Little Horn

Article Seven ............................................................... 99
   The Little Horn's Brutal Career

Article Eight ............................................................... 117
   Will the Tribulation Begin with a Peace Treaty?

Article Nine ................................................................ 133
   The Prophecy That Satan Feared

Article Ten ................................................................. 147
   The Prophecy That Answered Daniel's Questions

Article Eleven ........................................................................165
   Time, Times, and Half a Time
Article Twelve .........................................................................191
   Iron and Clay Mixed
Before the End .......................................................................203
   Daniel — A Prophetic Life
The End ....................................................................................211
   In the Lion's Den

# Other Books by Nelson Walters:

*Are We Ready for Jesus (2015)*

*Revelation Deciphered (2016)*

*Rapture: Case Closed? (2017)*

*Simplifying the Rapture (2018)*

*70 Times 7 (2018)*

*How To Prepare For the Last Days (2019)*

*Dawn of A New Day (2019)*

# Visit Us:

## The Gospel in the End Times Ministries

*www.thegospelintheendtimes.com*

nelson@thegospelintheendtimes.com

## Our YouTube Channel

www.youtube.com/channel/UCuWdmbJT3t7oCn5Puy7BmTQ/videos

We have over 60 original videos on end times theology, (most under 15 minutes in length)

# Article One

## What Are the Implications If Daniel Was Sealed?

Why read yet another commentary on Daniel? I mean, hasn't everything worth saying been said already? I think these are fair questions. From Hippolytus, to the Protestant reformers and Walvoord, the secrets of Daniel have been well documented. Haven't they?

But before you close this book and set it on your shelf, please consider with me a single verse from Daniel's last chapter:

> *But as for you, Daniel,* **conceal these words and seal up the book** *until the end of time; many will go back and forth, and knowledge will increase.* **(Dan 12:4, emphasis mine)**

Daniel was instructed to hide the words of his prophecies and seal the book for the end times. In the spiritual realm, I imagine Daniel and the angel placing this book of his prophecies in a large jar, the type similar to those used in Qumran to protect the Dead Sea scrolls from the desert heat. The prophet then sealed it, and it has laid dusty and untouched in a corner of heaven for 2,500 years.

What does this mean in the natural realm? Obviously, the physical words of the book of Daniel have been in the canon of scripture from the beginning. But have the *spiritual understanding* of the words been there? I'm sure you would agree with me that we can only understand a book of the Bible with the help of the Holy Spirit:

## What Are the Implications If Daniel Was Sealed?

> *But a natural man does not accept the things of the Spirit of God, for they are foolishness to him; and he cannot understand them, because they are spiritually appraised.* **(1 Cor 2:14)**

If the book was supernaturally sealed, which is what Dan 12:4 suggests, did the Holy Spirit intentionally avoid assisting us with our understanding of the scriptural meaning of the words? Even though giants of the faith like the reformers and Walvoord read the book, did they fail to ascertain what it truly meant because they unknowingly did so without the Spirit?

Now this doesn't mean for one moment that these men weren't spiritually-led and wonderfully-gifted in all other areas of their lives as teachers and expositors. Heaven forbid! But in this one area, in this one book of the Bible, did they fail to understand because its meaning could only be *spiritually appraised*?

Then in the fullness of time, sometime after Walvoord, did Jesus lift the jar above his head and smash it to the ground — effectively *unsealing* the book? If so, does the Holy Spirit now assist us in understanding the deep spiritual meaning of the prophecies? That is my belief. And shortly I will explain why I think that way, and why I believe it was previously sealed.

If I am correct, then there was never a more important time to read a new commentary on Daniel. And never was there more at stake. So, I invite you to consider this book as my humble attempt to communicate what I believe the Spirit has been saying to me about Daniel. As Daniel has said, this is my attempt at *one voice going back and forth* (Dan 12:4).

You see, I am highly encouraged by the last part of Dan 12:4, the part about *many will go back and forth, and knowledge will increase.*

Because this is not an individual effort. The Word says *many* will go back and forth from Daniel (now that it has been unsealed) to other books of the Bible, to help make sense of all of prophecy. It is a team effort. As believers, we are all in this together. And only the *many* will bring about the increase of knowledge that we desire and require.

## The Third Book of Articles

I'm sure this early discussion has left you with many questions, but before we begin to answer them, I'd like to take a brief moment to describe to you what type of book this is. It actually is the third book of this type that I have published — a book derived from the transcripts of many of the popular videos on my YouTube Channel. So, it is more properly classified as a collection of articles than a book of chapters.

The first book, *How to Prepare for the Last Days* (2019), began as a full-length instructional video about the last days. It was itself a collection of a dozen individual videos. The second book, *Dawn of a New Day* (2019), was somewhat broader in focus and is a collection of articles that had their beginnings as transcripts in 20-plus videos about the Tribulation, the rapture, the Second Coming, the wrath of God, and just about everything else you might want to understand about what scripture has to say about these and other critical end times events. If you haven't already done so, I encourage you to look for these books. I believe you will find their teachings to be both innovative and highly enlightening.

## What Are the Implications If Daniel Was Sealed?

Figure 1-1

This third book, *Daniel Unsealed* (2019), focuses entirely on the prophecies within the book of Daniel — the central prophetic book of the Bible, upon which most other prophecies are based. *Daniel Unsealed* is filled with new interpretations and insights based on the Daniel prophecies.

Make no mistake: If you are even a little bit concerned about your last days on earth and your eternal future, then this is a book you must read. And you must share it with those you love and with those in your church.

## What if Daniel Hasn't Been Unsealed?

This section asks a question that should deeply disturb most Christians. If the book of Daniel is still supernaturally sealed, what prophesies can we trust? Are there any in the entire Bible? Because many other prophecies are based on Daniel, if Daniel's prophecies are sealed, many other prophecies may be, as well.

## Daniel Unsealed

We have already looked at Dan 12:4. But if we look closer, we find that Daniel wasn't given the instruction to seal this book in just this one verse. It turns out that the instruction was given three times: In Dan 12:4, in Dan 12:9, and again in Dan 8:26. Three times the angel instructed Daniel to keep the words of his prophecy sealed and secret.

There are no exclamation points in Hebrew. In order for authors to emphasize a subject or topic in ancient writings, they simply repeated them multiple times. So, obviously, a three-time repetition would be considered extremely important. There is no doubt the book of Daniel was sealed.

This sealing is also unusual. Out of 66 books in the Canon of Scripture, only the book of Daniel was sealed. This means that of all the books of the Bible, we need only be primarily concerned with understanding the secrets hidden within this particular book.

I first became aware of this sealing about 25 years ago. A Jewish friend asked me about what was going to happen in the future, in the end times. And because he was Jewish, he and I chose to study an Old Testament book, Daniel. I thought it was a great opportunity to witness to him, as well. When we reached the portion of the 70 Weeks prophecy in Dan 9, I showed him how the Jewish Messiah had already come and died for his sins. Needless to say, this shocked him. My friend took his notes about Daniel to his rabbi whose short answer was, "The book is supernaturally sealed until the end times. We Jews don't read Daniel."

"That's odd," I thought. "They don't read the book that has the answers they need!"

## What Are the Implications If Daniel Was Sealed?

Christians, however, haven't been the slightest bit hesitant about studying Daniel. From the earliest Church fathers on, Christians have shared their ideas about what the prophet's various visions mean. But I want us to stop and think: Has this been wise or foolish?

If the real meanings of the prophecies in the book have been kept from us — if they've been sealed and hidden from us — is it possible that we've been inadvertently propagating false doctrine about the end times for centuries? Think about what this might mean. What if we've been wrong about one or more of the kingdoms in the dream of Nebuchadnezzar's statue? What about Chapter 7 and the vision of the four Beasts? Have we been wrong about that? Or what about Chapter 8, and the vision of the Ram and Goat? Could we have missed the proper meaning of that, as well?

Chapter 9 is all about the 70 Weeks prophecy. Is it possible we have also been wrong about what is arguably the most important prophecy in the Bible? What if the majority of the Church has been teaching erroneous interpretations about all of these prophecies — not because the teachers could not interpret them, but because the prophecies themselves were supernaturally sealed and were incapable of being understood? Where would that leave us?

Well, if the book of Daniel has truly been locked up and the meanings of the various prophecies have been kept from us, then we need to do some very deep thinking on the matter. Because this is not a trivial issue.

The first question we need to ask is this: Did Daniel have the right to seal the book? He was, after all, only a human. Yet we see throughout the Bible where God granted his prophets the right to perform incredible feats on His behalf. Moses parted the Red Sea at God's command. Ezekiel prophesied, and dry bones came to life on God's command. And, most certainly, God granted His prophets the right to record His Words. Would it really be that much more difficult to seal a book than to record it, if God willed it?

The second question concerns whether there is any precedent to God's Word being sealed. When we look, we find that of course the answer is *yes*. Within scripture, we find that, as a nation, Israel remains supernaturally hardened to the Gospel until the fullness of the Gentiles is fulfilled. This is still in effect. Isn't it also possible that the seal of Daniel is still in effect?

For the third question, we must ask ourselves this: If it turns out that the book of Daniel is still sealed, when will it be unsealed? When will its meanings start to be made known? We know from scripture that Daniel was advised by the angel exactly when this would be: He was told that the book would be sealed until the end times.

So, the follow-on question becomes, "What exactly are the end times, when do they occur, and is it possible that we may be in them already?" If we're not, then we need to be very careful about interpreting what the prophecies in Daniel mean, even today. And, just maybe, we need to remain silent about what we think Daniel's prophecies mean — because it's entirely possible that we don't really know! Better to be silent than to be wrong.

Now, some will say that we have been in the *last days* since Jesus's day. And guess what? They're right! The book of Hebrews tells us that the last days began with the First Coming

## What Are the Implications If Daniel Was Sealed?

of Jesus. The last 2,000 years are *all* the last days. But is that the same as the *end times*? We will explore that shortly.

There are others who will say that Daniel was unsealed when John wrote Revelation. We will discuss that possibility in just a little bit, as well. But, ultimately, I think we should let scripture interpret scripture for us. We shouldn't speculate. We should let the book of Daniel tell us when the end times are and when the time of the end occurs.

When we explore the prophecies in Daniel, we find a clear statement regarding the beginning of the end times. In Dan 8:17, and then again in Dan 8:19, the angel Gabriel told us three times. He repeated himself to clearly articulate how important this information was. Remember, there are no exclamation points in Hebrew:

> *"Son of man, understand that the vision pertains to the time of the end"* ... *"Behold, I am going to let you know what will occur at the final period of the indignation, for it pertains to the appointed time of the end."* **(Dan 8:17, 19)**

Gabriel told Daniel that the prophecies in Dan 8 would mark these three things: The beginning of the time of the end; the final indignation, or wrath of God; and the appointed time of the end, the return of our Lord.

The beginning of the prophecy in Dan 8 also marks the beginning of the time of the end. So *Dan 8 is the key*. If you want to understand more about the prophecy, Article Four in this book fully explains the biblical reasons why the end times have begun. But at this point, please accept my opinion that the prophecy and the end times have begun.

My guess is that the modern fulfillment of the beginning of Dan 8 occurred just within the past 35 to 40 years. So the end times began sometime around 1980. Now, you may scoff at this date and wonder how determining such a date is even possible. But I ask that you not cast judgment until you have read Article Four. You will be amazed, I promise you.

If that date is correct, then it's a classic *good news, bad news* scenario. The good news is that, in my opinion, Daniel is now unsealed, which means that believers can begin to understand it. The bad news is that every theory about the book of Daniel that was developed prior to 1980 may be in error! Shocking, I know.

## Implications of Daniel Being Unsealed

The fact that Daniel is now unsealed means we need to more closely examine all of our most treasured beliefs about the Daniel prophecies. It most likely also means that our most beloved Christian expositors may have been wrong in some respects about what they have taught about Daniel. Again, this has nothing to do with whether they were qualified or intelligent, or even whether they were Spirit-filled. It simply has to do with the fact that the book was sealed. *Nobody* — at least nobody human — was going to understand Daniel as long as it was sealed and its contents supernaturally hidden.

So, if a theory about a prophecy in Daniel is older than 40 years, I strongly suggest that you be very wary and re-examine it with fresh eyes. For example, if you believe that the legs of iron in Dan 2 are *Rome*, then you need to recognize that this is a very old idea, one that was developed long ago, while the book was still sealed. That doesn't mean that this theory is wrong; but it sure doesn't mean that it's correct. We completely re-examine this theory in Article Two.

## What Are the Implications If Daniel Was Sealed?

If you believe that Dan 8 is only about the war between Persia and Greece and was fulfilled long ago by Alexander the Great, that also is a very old idea, developed while Daniel was still sealed. We re-examine this theory in Article Four. Based strictly on the angel's statements that we've already mentioned, you can already imagine that this prophecy is about the time of the end, and not about history.

Additionally, if you think that the 70th Week of Daniel — or as it is sometimes called, *the Tribulation* — begins with a peace treaty, then you are believing in yet another theory that became popular while the book of Daniel was still sealed, during a time when it would not have been possible to properly understand it. So we also re-examine this theory later in the book, in Article Eight.

Wow! You're probably thinking to yourself, "If all of these ideas that I've had are mistaken, then I'm going to have to rethink everything I thought was true about the end times!" And *yes*, that is exactly what I have done personally, over the past 10 years. So welcome to the club!

Some readers may be unwilling to throw away their treasured theories at this point. I completely understand. For now, we ask only that you carefully reconsider what you may have long believed true about this particular scripture and leave yourself open to new understandings. Let us all pray for a filling of the Holy Spirit and His wisdom as we study these matters.

### Revelation and Daniel

Let's look briefly at the sealing of the book of Revelation, because this is quite interesting. John was specifically told *not* to seal up the book of Revelation.

# Daniel Unsealed

> *And he said to me, "Do not seal up the words of the prophecy of this book, for the time is near."* **(Rev 22:10)**

Why was John instructed not to seal this book? There is no other book in the Bible for which an instruction was given to *not seal it up*.

Revelation contains things about Daniel's prophecies that were sealed at the time of John's writing. So, anything we read about Daniel in the book of Revelation has been unsealed. I assume John was specifically instructed not to seal Revelation so that everyone reading it would be able to understand the things in it that referred to Daniel.

Additionally, we know that anything that Jesus taught us about Daniel's prophecies in the Gospels have also been unsealed for the last 2,000 years. The Gospels are a good source of unsealed information about Daniel.

And for any of you out there still doubting that the book of Daniel was sealed, the instructions of the angel to John to *not seal* the book of Revelation should be proof enough that Daniel was sealed. Why else would the angel instruct John to *not seal* Revelation?

## The Unsealing of Daniel

Finally, let's return to the sealing of Daniel. If we look at the actual wording, it says:

> *As for you Daniel, conceal these words and seal up the book until the time of the end. Many will go back and forth and knowledge will increase.* **(Dan 12:4)**

## What Are the Implications If Daniel Was Sealed?

Look specifically at that last phrase. The words *many will go back and forth* may be referring to going back and forth between the book of Daniel and other books in the Bible — like Revelation and the Gospels — in order to gain further knowledge. Now that Daniel is unsealed, it has opened up the potential to understand vast portions of scripture which were based on Daniel.

As I mentioned previously, I am also encouraged by the word *many* in this passage. This is a group project! All Christians are empowered by the Holy Spirit, and all of us have a responsibility to see that the prophecies are fully unsealed and understood.

I must admit that I am offended by prophetic teachers who suffer from what is called the *Prophet Syndrome*. This is a malady in which the teacher believes that God only speaks to him or her. That's just nonsense! The Holy Spirit speaks to *all* Christians. And He speaks through the Holy Word. We're all in this together!

### Why was Daniel Sealed?

We have held the most difficult question for last. How can someone know the mind of the Almighty? How can we know why Daniel was sealed? If it isn't revealed to us, we can't.

We can only guess at God's motives. Why would He unseal the prophecies only in the end times? Perhaps, because that is when they will be needed. Perhaps because it was considered that, prior to the end times, knowledge of what will happen during that period was just *interesting information* — nice to know, but not crucial. But during the end times, application of the correct understanding may be the difference between life and death.

I can only speak for myself. The knowledge that Daniel was sealed and now has been unsealed has caused me to search the prophecies and study them with a fervor. I would never have undertaken the intense study I have if I thought that it was *business-as-usual* and that others had done all the heavy-lifting for me.

The unsealing of Daniel has also left me with the calling to *share* what I know with others.

> *Those who have insight among the people will give understanding to the many.* **(Dan 11:33)**

And in the process, others have taught me. It is this process of the *many going back and forth* through which knowledge is indeed increasing.

In conclusion, the book of Daniel has most likely been unsealed within the last 40 years. Now is the time to join me and fellow believers in a Holy quest for truth. Let's study Daniel like never before, as if our very lives depended on it. Because quite frankly, they probably do.

# Article Two

## Will the Fourth Kingdom Be Rome or the Islamic Caliphate?

God gave King Nebuchadnezzar of Babylon a dream that Christians have studied and debated for years. In the dream, God showed the King a statue that represented the governments and kingdoms of the world right up until the glorious return of Jesus. A few questions remain unanswered, however — the most salient of which is this: Is the fourth kingdom Rome, or is it the Islamic Caliphate?

This article is about Dan 2 and the dream of the great statue, because everything that follows in this book is built upon what we discover about this statue. Until the year 2006, there wasn't much of a question as to what kingdoms made up the parts of the great statue in this vision. Nearly every Christian scholar up to that point assumed that the fourth kingdom of the statue was Rome. It was an open and closed case — so much so that many Bible translations of that day included section headers that claimed the fourth kingdom was Rome. Those words weren't actually found in the text; they were headings added by the translators to help readers *understand* the text. My NASB Bible has a heading titled *Rome*.

But approximately 14 years ago, all that changed with the publication of the blockbuster book *Islamic Antichrist*, by my good friend Joel Richardson. In that book, Richardson asserted that the Antichrist will be Islamic, not Roman. And in his subsequent book, *Mideast Beast*, he followed up the initial analysis with detailed biblical exegesis that set the world of biblical scholarship on fire; and the question of whether the Antichrist will be Roman or Islamic has been debated worldwide ever since.

## The King's Dream

A major part of this debate centered on the interpretation of Nebuchadnezzar's dream of a statue and the arguments about which nation was the fourth kingdom. The reason for the debate is that during the dream and the subsequent explanation by the prophet Daniel, we are *never actually told* the names of the various kingdoms. Scholars have had to infer them from clues provided in the text.  So let's look at the various arguments presented, so that you will be better able to make up your own mind on this issue. And if you're not familiar with this prophecy, we'll give you the abbreviated version to get you up to speed.

God gave King Nebuchadnezzar of Babylon a dream which scared the King, because he knew it was very important.  He called on his advisors and wise men to help him understand it. But rather than simply asking them what the dream meant, Nebuchadnezzar wisely asked them to tell him what the dream was about, and *then* what it meant. He rightly suspected that he might get just any answer if he asked *only* what the dream meant; but he knew that if one or more of his advisors could *first* tell him what the dream was about, then he had a better chance of receiving an accurate interpretation of the *meaning* of the dream.

The wise men and astrologers couldn't tell him about the dream. They were dumbfounded. They responded to the King:

> *The thing which the King demands is difficult and there is no one else who could declare it to the king except the gods.* **(Dan 2:11)**

The King was enraged and declared that if they didn't tell him what the dream and its interpretation meant, all of the wise men would be killed, including Daniel. The wise men were correct in believing that only God could disclose the dream and its meaning.

Now Daniel, who had just completed his training to be one of the wise men, sought the Lord; and God provided Daniel an understanding of the dream and its interpretation. Daniel told the King:

> *There is a God in heaven who reveals mysteries and he has made known to King Nebuchadnezzar what will take place in the latter days.* **(Dan 2:27)**

Daniel revealed that the statue which appeared in the King's dream was comprised of *five layers*, each made of a *different material* and each representing a *different kingdom*: A head of *gold*, a chest and arms of *silver*, a belly and thighs of *bronze*, legs of *iron*, and feet and toes of *iron mixed with clay*. In the dream, the statue was struck by a *stone*, which then crushed all portions of the statue at the same time. After it crushed the statue, the stone grew to be a mountain that filled the whole world.

The *stone* is Jesus, who will crush the kingdoms of this world upon His triumphant return. Since the feet and toes of the statue — which represent the final kingdom according to Daniel's interpretation — will be the portion of the statue struck when Jesus returns at the Second Coming, they must be representative of the realm of the Antichrist.

Therefore, knowing the identity of the kingdom of *iron* — which is connected directly to the toes — will help us to identify the kingdom of the Antichrist.

## The Layers of the Statue

Let's examine this prophecy in more detail to see what we can learn from the interpretation Daniel was given by God. Daniel first told the King that he, Nebuchadnezzar, was the head of *gold*. About the second kingdom, Daniel said that, after Nebuchadnezzar, another kingdom would arise which will be inferior. This is the chest and arms of *silver*. Daniel then advised that a third kingdom of *bronze* would subsequently replace the second kingdom.

Before we begin to look at the *fourth kingdom*, which is the topic of this article, let's consider what we've learned so far. It's important that Daniel told the King that the first kingdom was Babylon. It was made of *gold*, and it was the head. About this kingdom Daniel told the king:

> *You, O king, are the king of kings, to whom the God of heaven has given the kingdom, the power, the strength and the glory; and wherever the sons of men dwell, or the Beasts of the field, or the birds of the sky, He has given them into your hand and has caused you to rule over them all.* **(Dan 2:37-38)**

The entire prophecy concerns this kingdom. The land of Babylon was given to Nebuchadnezzar, but not forever. It would later pass to subsequent empires, and to rulers of other nations.

Our English translations say that the kingdom, or possibly *kingdoms,* that followed Babylon would be inferior to it. So, what might this mean? One thing it doesn't mean is that Babylon was larger or more powerful than the kingdom that followed. Here is a map representing the greatest expansion achieved by the Babylonian Empire:

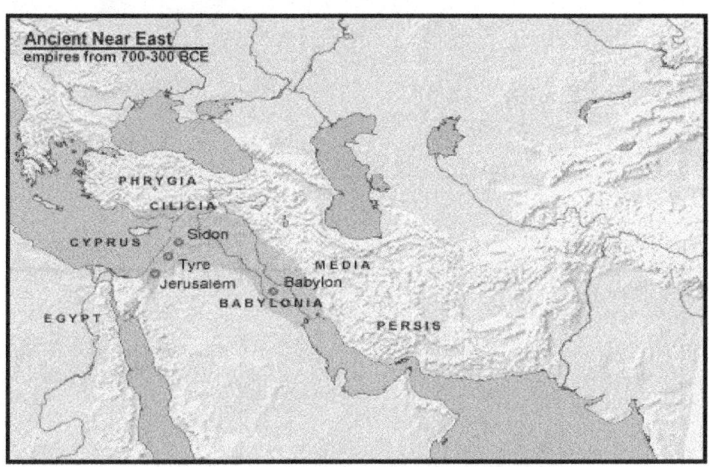

Figure 2-1

Persia, the next empire, and represented by the arms and the chest of *silver*, was substantially larger than Babylon. And Greece, the third empire, was larger still. Size alone did not determine what made one kingdom greater than another. So, why was the subsequent kingdom(s) considered *inferior*?

The following two figures are maps representing the largest extents of the Empires of Persia and Greece (Macedonia):

## Will the Fourth Kingdom Be Rome or the Islamic Caliphate?

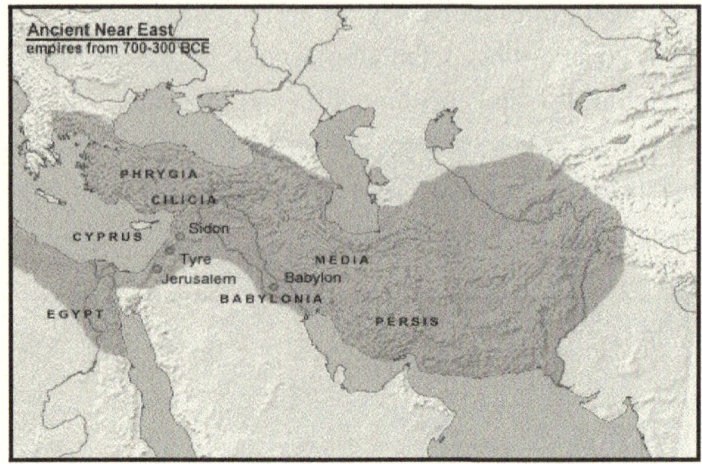

Figure 2-2

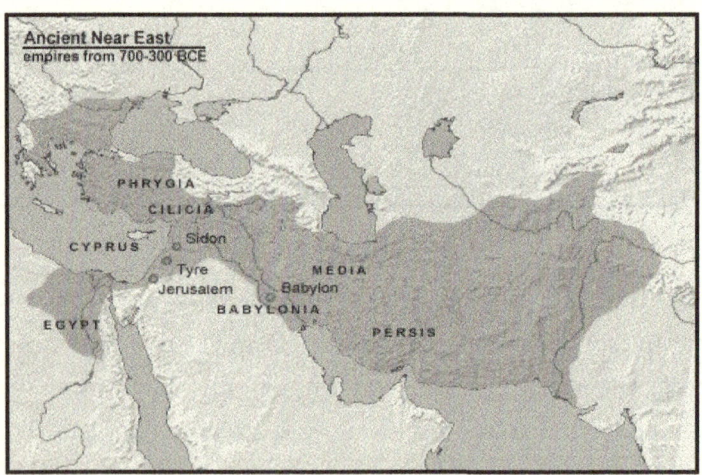

Figure 2-3

The shocking answer is that, in my opinion, the other kingdom(s) — one or more — *weren't* inferior to Babylon. The literal text of the Bible doesn't say that they were. To which, I'm sure you're thinking, "Well, my Bible clearly says *inferior*, and we know the Bible is infallible." The Bible is, but translators aren't.

The Hebrew word translated *inferior* in most English translations doesn't mean that at all! This Hebrew word, *ara*, is found 20 times in the scriptures, and in *every other occurrence* it means *land or earth*. Daniel used the same word just two verses earlier to say that Babylon filled the whole *earth*. And in the very next verse, he used this same Hebrew word to say that the bronze kingdom would rule the whole *earth*.

So, doesn't it make sense that in all of these cases, the prophecy is speaking of the *same* territory? And that territory is *Babylon*!

The very next Hebrew word found in Dan 2:39 is *minnak*, which literally means *out from*. So, together these two words literally mean *out from your land*; and a better translation of what this verse is actually saying might be:

> *Another Kingdom shall arise after you* **out of your earth (or out of your land.)** *And yet a third kingdom of bronze shall rule over all the earth (or land.)* **(Dan 2:39, translation mine)**

This makes so much more sense than most of our English translations! The verse is talking about the *land mass* of Babylon and who will rule it in the future. *This is an important understanding.*

In fact, it may be the single greatest key to understanding the identity of the fourth kingdom and to establishing why that identity has remained a mystery until recently. So, let's state it again: God told Daniel the interpretation, and that interpretation was that Babylon would rule the *known earth* at that time. And then subsequent kingdoms would rule the *same territory*.

# Will the Fourth Kingdom Be Rome or the Islamic Caliphate?

Looking at the maps of Babylon, Persia, and Greece, we can see this is true. It stands to reason, then, that the fourth kingdom — the one which came after these others — will also rule this same territory. That, in my opinion, is what the prophecy of the Statue is all about. It's about the land or the territory. And that territory was *Babylon*.

## Is Rome the Fourth Kingdom?

So, you probably think we're now ready to discuss Rome's control of the land mass that was Babylon, which will prove that the fourth kingdom is Rome, right? Well, not exactly.

When the Greek Empire dissolved, the land mass that was Babylon was divided. Rome controlled the western portion of the land, which included Turkey, Syria, and Israel. The Parthian Empire controlled the Babylonian motherland to the east. Neither the Roman nor the Parthian Empires can be considered the fourth kingdom, because neither controlled *all* of the Babylonian territory. Remember, the prophecy is about the *territory*.

The following is a map of the Roman and Parthian Empires:

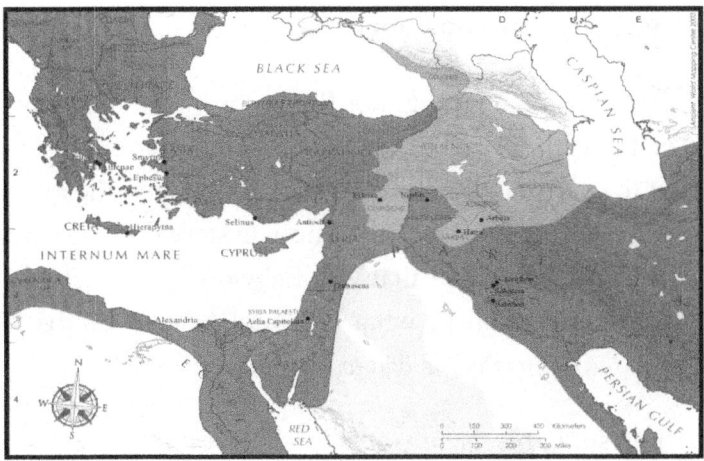

Figure 2-4

At this point, you may be asking yourself, "Is he saying that Rome never controlled Babylon? That can't be. I've seen maps clearly showing that it did." Well, you may have seen maps indicating this, but those maps are mistaken, for all periods except for a *single year*.

The Roman Emperor Trajan attacked and entered the city of Babylon in AD 115, but he left soon thereafter and died of a stroke while returning to Rome. His son and successor, Hadrian, then became Emperor and abandoned most of the Middle East, including Babylon. Rome held Babylon for only *one year*. That hardly counts as making it part of the Roman Empire!

The maps you referred to likely showed the greatest extent of the Roman Empire, which included the single year in which it occupied Babylon. My personal opinion is that maps displaying Babylon as part of the Roman Empire may exist largely because, without them, those who otherwise believe Rome is the fourth kingdom would have nothing to support their position.

### Will the Fourth Kingdom Be Rome or the Islamic Caliphate?

## Was the Caliphate the Fourth Kingdom?

Neither the Parthian Empire nor Rome controlled the entire land mass of Babylon. So, what was the fourth kingdom? Who was the next to control it? You probably already know the answer: It was the Islamic Caliphate. The Caliphate started by Mohammed conquered all of the land that was Babylon by AD 670. And by the strictest definition of what it would take to be the fourth kingdom, *the Caliphate was that fourth kingdom*.

Now, I'm sure this is not at all what you've been taught. I understand that. The reason your teachers have presented a different view may be that most of them — and the rest of us — have always looked at world history from the perspective of Europe, or maybe Israel. But Dan 2 is about Nebuchadnezzar's dream, and the Spirit-led interpretation of that dream came from the perspective of Babylon — not Europe, and certainly not Israel. But, of course, the conquering of the land isn't the only proof that the fourth kingdom is the Caliphate.

As we continue to look at the text of Dan 2, we will understand better what it says about the fourth kingdom. Does it support the theory that it was the Caliphate, or does it support Rome? We are given one major clue: In Dan 2:40, we are told that this fourth kingdom will break and shatter all the kingdoms that came before it.

Did Rome break and shatter the empires that came before it? We already know that it didn't break or crush the land masses. It held Babylon for one year and never even entered Persia. Did it crush Greek culture and substitute its own? Not even close. In fact, Rome copied Greek architecture and worshipped gods surprisingly similar to those in Greece, just with different names. Furthermore, Romans used Greek as the language of commerce and business. So you see, Rome didn't *crush* Greek culture or the cultures of other captured nations, it *adopted* them.

But what about Islam? Islamic invaders *crushed* the cultures they invaded. Not only did they crush and capture the geography of all the previous kingdoms, they forced their monotheistic god, Allah, on the conquered peoples at the point of a sword. They instituted new architecture and the Arabic language. And, above all, they forced their Sharia law and calendars on their foes, thereby changing the laws and the seasons in the conquered territories. Islam means *submission*, and the Caliphate forced captives to submit to the Islamic culture. Islam is a much, much better match for the Bible's description of the fourth kingdom than Rome. Not only does the rise of the Islamic Caliphate match scriptures about the fourth kingdom better than Rome, its demise does as well.

Daniel told us that Jesus will break into pieces all five kingdoms represented by the statue upon His return — all at the same time. That's easy to visualize with Islam. If the Caliphate is revived, it will include all of Babylon, Persia, and Greece. All will be destroyed at the same time that the Caliphate is destroyed. But this would not be true of Rome, as it did not include all of Babylon; and it included none of the Persian Empire.

If we look at it honestly, we realize that there is really nothing to support Rome as the fourth kingdom. Nothing. To which you might say, "Wait a minute, wasn't Rome the *fourth* kingdom in the *historical sequence*? Didn't it control the land right after Greece?"

Unfortunately, this popular theory isn't true either. The Seleucid Empire, not the Roman Empire, replaced Greece. It was the

## Will the Fourth Kingdom Be Rome or the Islamic Caliphate?

fourth in time, if you count the Seleucids as a separate empire. And, frankly, the Romans weren't even the *fifth* kingdom. The Parthian Empire existed for over a hundred years prior to the Romans. They were the fifth in time; Rome was *sixth*.

Let's look at the final physical aspect of Nebuchadnezzar's dream, the *feet and toes,* and see if there is a fit with either Islam or Rome. We are told by Daniel that the final, fifth kingdom will be a divided kingdom. No kingdom on earth has ever been more divided than Islam. The divide between *Sunni and Shia* is deeper than just land or politics; it is about which one is the proper Muslim religion. This divide cuts to the very soul of Islam. No divide in a revived Roman Empire could ever be as deep.

The Bible attests to the divided and conflicted nature of the Arab people within themselves:

> *You shall call his name Ishmael, because the Lord has given heed to your affliction. He will be a wild donkey of a man, his hand will be against everyone, and everyone's hand will be against him; and he will live to the east of all his brothers.* **(Gen 16:11-12)**

So, in each and every aspect that we have looked at, Rome is a very poor second to the Islamic Caliphate as a candidate to be the *legs of iron,* the *fourth kingdom* of Nebuchadnezzar's statue. The reason Rome has dominated in discussions of this topic in Western nations is most certainly because Europeans and their descendants have been the ones having those discussions! Rome has had a central place in the development of Europe. It is therefore the first to come to mind when discussing historic conquests and national expansion. Moreover, hatred among

Protestants for the Roman Catholic Church has further pushed the Rome position to the forefront.

However, if we look at the various options biblically and with the retrospective eye of history, it becomes clear that only the *Islamic Caliphate* meets the scriptural criteria to be the *fourth kingdom*.

# Article Three

## The Beast from the Sea in Daniel 7

The *Beast from the sea*: Even the name conjures up fear. Daniel devotes an entire chapter in Dan 7, to this monster. And when Daniel was done speaking of him, he told us the color left his face, and he felt weak. John mentions this same Beast over 30 times in Revelation. When we combine what we learn from Daniel and Revelation, we are left with the Bible's most complete picture of this coming horror.

The Beast from the sea in Dan 7 may be the focus of that chapter, but when most of us think about the chapter, it's the *four Beasts* that most people think of first. They're so exotic — with wings and multiple heads — that the *terrifying Beast* is somehow pushed to the background. Because of this, most Bible studies of Dan 7 begin with a study of the four Beasts. But, guess what? We're taking a very different approach. We're going to focus first on this terrifying, *fourth Beast*. And for two very good reasons:

First, because John focuses on this Beast in Rev 13 and Rev 17 and mostly ignores the others. And second, because the fourth Beast is a *composite* of the first three Beasts:

> And the Beast which I saw was like a Leopard, and his feet were like those of a Bear, and his mouth like the mouth of a Lion. **(Rev 13:2)**

When we study the fourth Beast, we learn about *all* of them.

## The Nature of the Beast

The angel that explained the vision to Daniel said that the four Beasts are four kings. Therefore, the final Beast is a both a man and a king. This is reinforced by what Paul writes about him in 2 Thess, calling him a man of lawlessness or sin:

> *Let no one in any way deceive you, for it will not come unless the apostasy comes first, and the man of lawlessness is revealed, the son of destruction, who opposes and exalts himself above every so-called god or object of worship, so that he takes his seat in the temple of God, displaying himself as being God.* **(2 Thess 2:3-4)**

In Isa 14 there is a reference to the Antichrist, and we learn that he is a man who overthrows the cities of the world:

> *They will ponder over you, saying, "Is this the man who made the earth tremble, who shook kingdoms?"* **(Isa 14:16)**

In addition to being a *man*, we are told that the Beast is *also* a *kingdom*:

> *He said: 'The fourth Beast will be a fourth kingdom on the earth, which will be different from all the other kingdoms and will devour the whole earth and tread it down and crush it.'* **(Dan 7:23)**

Moreover, in addition to being a kingdom and a man, the Beast will *also be a demon*, one who rises out of the bottomless pit, or abyss:

> *The Beast that comes up out of the abyss will make war with them, and overcome them and kill them.* **(Rev 11:7)**

The *abyss* is a term that is used exclusively in scripture as a holding place for demons. Humans go to the grave, or *Sheol*. In Luke 8, Jesus cast out demons from a man known as Legion. The demons then begged Jesus not to send them into the abyss. So, Jesus sent them into a herd of pigs instead. Satan himself will be chained in the abyss after the return of Jesus. These examples reinforce the idea that the abyss a holding area for evil spirits.

Jude and Peter both allude to this place where evil spirits are kept in chains awaiting judgment:

> *And angels who did not keep their own domain, but abandoned their proper abode, He has kept in eternal bonds under darkness for the judgment of the great day.* **(Jude 1:6)**

> *For if God did not spare angels when they sinned, but cast them into hell and committed them to pits of darkness, reserved for judgment.* **(2 Pet 2:4)**

However, it seems at least one demon is released: *The Beast*. We will discuss what demon this might be later in this article.

Daniel clearly tells us that the Antichrist will not act on his own, but, rather, will receive help from a *foreign god*. This is the demonic aspect of the Beast, I believe:

> *He will take action against the strongest of fortresses with the help of a foreign god.* **(Dan 11:39)**

In my teaching ministry I constantly hear disagreements about the *nature of the Beast*. Many argue it's a demon. Others say it's a kingdom. Still others believe it's a man. I agree with *all three*. All three are right, and we have been arguing in circles about this point.

However, there appears to be an order to the process by which the Beast becomes a three-part entity. It seems to begin as a kingdom under the authority of 10 kings:

> *As for the 10 horns, out of this kingdom 10 kings will arise; and another will arise after them.* **(Dan 7:24)**

Only after this kingdom is established and the 10 kings arise does the man known variously as Little Horn, the Man of Sin, and the Antichrist make his presence known.

And, after he appears, the demonic aspect of the Beast arises from the bottomless pit and possesses the man who is king of this kingdom. This is a *very important understanding*: That the *Beast is man, kingdom, and demon*, all at the same time. When we read the term *Beast* in our Bibles, either in Daniel or in Revelation, we need to remember that it could be referring to the man, to the kingdom, to the demon, or to all three. If we keep this in mind, it is less likely that we'll get tripped-up in interpretation. In fact, this is one of the *keys to understanding* this evil force. We need to keep this in mind at all times.

## The Beast Arises

Let's see what else Daniel has to say about how this evil force arises:

> *Daniel said I was looking in my vision at night and behold the four winds of heaven were stirring up the Great Sea.* **(Dan 7:2)**

We have two symbols that we need to understand from this passage: The *sea*, and the *four winds of heaven*. Let's begin with the sea. The angel in Revelation explains this symbol to John:

> *The waters which you saw where the harlot sits are peoples and multitudes and nations and tongues.* **(Rev 17:10)**

Therefore, the *sea or waters* are the nations, specifically the *Gentile nations*. Later in this chapter of Revelation, the sea is contrasted with the *land*, which is *Israel*. And if you remember from Dan 7, it was the *great sea* that the Beasts came out of. In the Old Testament, the great sea was the eastern Mediterranean.

If you are one of those who believes that the Beast will arise in either America or Europe, I want you consider that Daniel *specifically* informs us that the Beast arises from the *eastern Mediterranean*. This seems to eliminate both America and Europe as sources of the Beast.

Let's return to our symbols. The *four winds* are four angels, or four spirits. In fact, the Greek word for *winds* is the same as *spirits*. In Hebrews, we see that God makes his angels winds:

> *Of the angels he says, "He makes his angels winds."* **(Heb 1:7)**

And in the Old Testament book of Zechariah, the prophet sees four colored horses and asks what they are. He is told that they are going out to the four winds of heaven.

In combination, then, we've learned that the *four spirit beings* of God, the *four winds of heaven*, are stirring up the Gentile nations, specifically those along the eastern Mediterranean Sea. The four Beasts come out of that region. And, earlier, we also learned that the terrifying, fourth Beast is a combination of the first three Beasts. Let's look at that fourth Beast now in even greater detail.

## Description of the Beast

We are told in Revelation that this Beast has seven heads, 10 horns, and 10 diadem crowns on its horns:

> *I saw a Beast rising out of the sea, with 10 horns and seven heads, with 10 diadems on its horns and blasphemous names on its heads.* **(Rev 13:1)**

Believe it or not, the fact that the crowns are *on the horns* is important. Earlier in Revelation, we are introduced to Satan as a dragon with seven heads and 10 horns, just like the Beast. But there was a difference. Satan's crowns were *on* his *heads,* not on his horns. Later the crowns have moved to the horns of the Beast. What does this mean?

Diadem crowns are a sign of dominion and power. Throughout history, Satan has controlled the world through the seven heads. That's why the crowns are on his *heads*. It is evidence of his power and dominion over the earth. But, in the end times, Satan will *delegate* his dominion *to the 10 horns*. That's where the power will be. So even though power and dominion may have historically been associated with the heads, in the coming Beast Empire, these things will move to the horns. This is a *key understanding*.

We are told in scripture that the 10 horns are 10 kings and — as of John's day, in about AD 90 — those kings had not yet received their power. So, those who think that the 10 horns or kings were Roman emperors now have a real problem, because all of them would have had to receive power *after* AD 90!

Additionally, the 10 kings all receive power at the same time, together with the Beast, but for a very short period:

> *The 10 horns that you saw are 10 kings who have not yet received royal power but they are to receive authority as kings for one hour, together with the Beast.* **(Rev 17:12)**

They can't be emperors or popes for this reason. Emperor's and popes were successive rulers. These kings rule at one moment in time, and they rule along with the Beast. Moreover, the power they receive, they then *give to the Beast*:

> *These are of one mind, and they hand over their power and authority to the Beast.* **(Rev 17:13)**

Let's now consider the heads of the Beast. If the 10 horns are the *end times* holders of dominion and power, then the seven heads of Satan are the *historic* holders of power. That is where the crowns are found on Satan: On these heads.

Rev 17 helps us to identify these heads, these historic empires. The heads are the same on Satan and on the Beast. They are the seven empires or kingdoms associated with Satan's pursuit of the woman, who is Israel in Rev 12. We are also told that they are seven mountains and seven kings:

> *The seven heads are seven mountains on which the woman sits, and they are seven kings.* **(Rev 17:9-10)**

Mountain is a term the Bible often uses to describe a *kingdom*. Remember in our study in Dan 2 where the stone (God's Kingdom) became a mountain or a great kingdom? If *mountain* is a symbol of a kingdom, then each of the seven kingdoms must be associated with a king. The *seven heads are seven kingdoms and seven kings*. That makes sense.

## The Beast From the Sea in Daniel 7

This brings us to one of the most *persistent errors* in all of eschatology. Almost daily I hear these mountains referred to as *seven hills* — as in the seven hills of Rome. They are mountains, not hills. The underlying Greek word is *oros*, and it means *mountain, not hill*. This word is translated as mountain 63 times in the New Testament. So, in this case, as well as in all the others, it means mountain. Here is a breakdown of the etymology:

- *Original Word:* ὄρος, ους, τό

- *Part of Speech:* noun, neuter

- *Transliteration:* oros

- *Phonetic Spelling:* or'-os

- *Definition:* a mountain

The primary source of the error may be the NIV Bible, which mis-translates *oros* as hills. Based on this translation, it is possible that the NIV team of translators had a pre-existing bias toward a Roman Beast. But most English Bibles do translate it properly.

What we've learned so far is that the seven heads of Satan and the Beast are seven empires with seven kings that existed in the past, and that these empires pursued the woman who is Israel. But how can we identify these heads?

The angel tells us directly. He tells us that as of John's day in approximately AD 90, five empires had fallen or passed into history and that one remains (*is*). That means it was existing *in John's day*:

> *Five have fallen, one is, the other has not yet come; and when he comes, he must remain a little while.* **(Rev 17:10)**

It follows, then, that the existing head, this sixth head, was Rome, which clearly was the power in existence during John's day. We also understand that five of the empires had existed and passed from power prior to Rome. This is *important information*.

The angel then tells us that there will be one more head or empire *after* Rome. This seventh empire will last a fairly long time — it will have to remain *a little while*.

So, let's see if we can figure out what kingdoms are represented by the heads from this information. It really isn't that hard. We have already established that the sixth head is *Rome*. So let's work backwards from there and try to determine the previous five heads or empires that persecuted Israel or God's people.

The next preceding empire was *Greece*, or the Hellenistic Empire. Before that it was *Persia*, and before that *Babylon*. Prior to Babylon, *Assyria* persecuted Israel, and before that it was *Egypt*.

That only leaves one head or empire, the one *after* Rome, the one that has to last *a little while*, and the one that has persecuted God's people for centuries. This has to be the *Islamic Caliphate*, which existed from 600 AD to 1924, when it was beheaded, so to speak, by the Allied forces after WWI.

Scripture tells us about this particular head. Revelation says John saw one of the heads *as if* it had been *slain* — not that it was actually slain, but *as if* it had been slain. This is what happened to the Islamic Caliphate in 1924. The Allied army split the Ottoman Caliphate into a number of countries that now make up the Middle East, including Syria, Turkey, Iran, and Iraq:

> *I saw one of his heads as if it had been slain, and his fatal wound was healed. And the whole earth was amazed and followed after the Beast.* **(Rev 13:3)**

Scripture then tells us that this head will be *healed*. The angel told John that the world was amazed at this healing and followed after the Beast. So, in my opinion, the Islamic Caliphate will *rise again*. I think we are already seeing this beginning to happen, and ISIS represents the first attempt to reestablish it. Thus far, the efforts of ISIS have succeeded in stirring up interest within Islam for religious and political changes on a much grander scale.

Let's take a moment to compare the five kingdoms of Nebuchadnezzar's statue to what we have learned about the kingdoms that make up the 10 heads of the Beast:

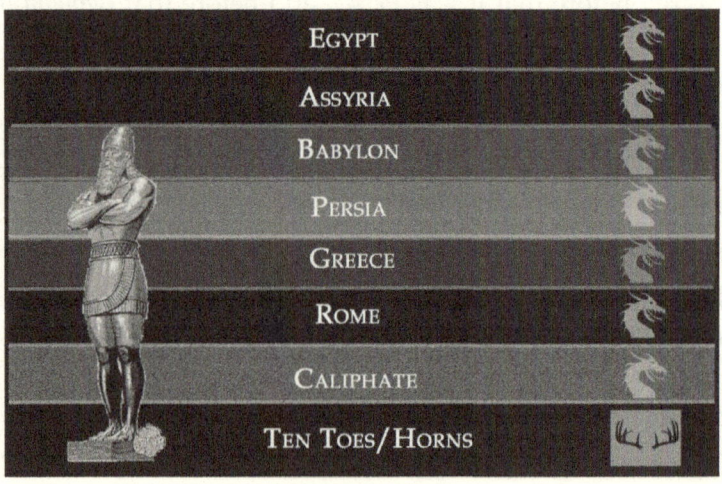

**Figure 3-1**

## Daniel Unsealed

The first thing we notice is that the statue has a fewer number of *layers* than the Beast has. It has only *five* layers, while the Beast has *eight*; seven heads, and then the horns. The reason for this difference is that the statue is from the perspective of Nebuchadnezzar, King of Babylon, while the Beast is from the perspective of God's people, Israel. So if you've ever wondered why Daniel and Revelation have *different* numbers of kingdoms, this is the reason.

There are three kingdoms that just about everyone agrees about in terms of position: *Babylon* is the head of gold; *Persia* is the chest of silver; and the Hellenistic kingdoms, or what we commonly call *Greece*, is the belly and thighs of bronze. In addition, nearly everyone agrees on the two empires that persecuted God's people prior to Nebuchadnezzar and Babylon: *Egypt* and *Assyria*. They aren't found on the statue, however, because they *preceded Babylon*. This leaves us with *three kingdoms that have or will persecute God's people*.

Next, let's fill in the final kingdom that is common to both the statue and Revelation's depiction of the Beast: The 10 toes and the 10 horns. These are the end times manifestation of the *Beast*.

That leaves us with *two* empires. We've learned from Revelation that the *sixth head*, the one that *is* during John's lifetime is Rome. Notice that this empire is *not* the legs of iron, as is so commonly taught. Rather, as we learned in the previous article, this empire is the *Islamic Caliphate*. We have provided multiple reasons why Rome was not the legs of iron or even part of Nebuchadnezzar's statue.

The *seventh head* of the Beast is the kingdom that defeated Rome in AD 1453 and came after it: the *Islamic Caliphate*. This is the kingdom that, per Revelation, appeared to suffer a fatal head wound and that most likely will come back to life.

Let's take a moment to consider what a kingdom would look like if it contained all of these other constituent kingdoms. It would probably look just like the fullest extent of the *Ottoman Caliphate*, the Empire whose head received the fatal wound in 1924!

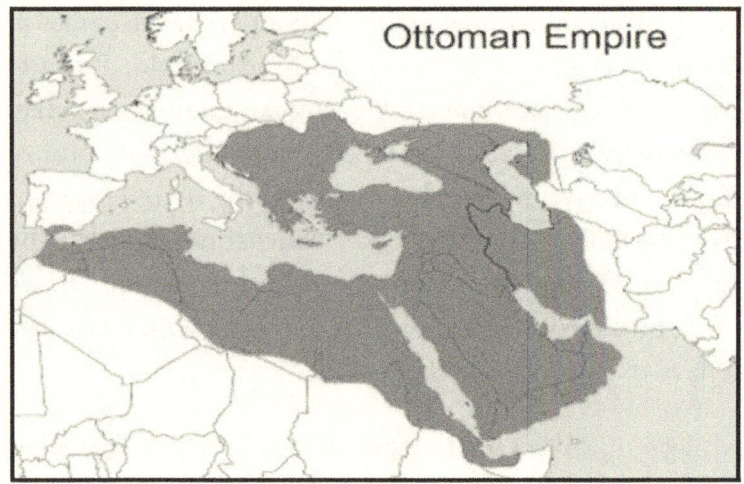

Figure 3-2

Are we looking at a *near-approximation* of the *Beast's Empire* of the 10 kings when it first arises? Maybe we are.

Now, many of you may be wondering how Rome can be included as one of the heads of the Beast, while Italy is wholly excluded from the map of the Beast's anticipated territories. As we mentioned earlier, a large part of the Roman Empire *is* included: The eastern Byzantine Roman Empire comprises a third of this area. Beyond that, we acknowledge only that the map represents the *actual* Ottoman Empire or Caliphate, which may or may not be identical to the coming empire of the Beast.

## Rise of the Little Horn

After the formation of the empire under the control of the 10 kings, the Little Horn comes on the scene:

> *While he was contemplating the horns behold another horn a little one came up among them.* **(Dan 7:8)**

For everyone who thinks they know who the Antichrist will be already, you can *forget speculating*. He comes up *after* the 10 horns, and they haven't even formed yet.

The Little Horn is the *man portion of the Beast*. He will become the visible representation of the Beast. He is the *Man of Sin*, who will sit in the Temple and eventually rule the Beast Empire. But he doesn't start out that way. At first, he is a *Little Horn*, almost an insignificant horn:

> *In his place a despicable person will arise, on whom the honor of kingship has not been conferred, but he will come in a time of tranquility and seize the kingdom by intrigue.* (Dan 11:21)

We see from Dan 11 that he is called a *despicable person*, who arises and upon whom the honor of kingship has not been conferred. So, if you are thinking this Little Horn is Trump, Obama, Marcon, or the pope, all of whom could be considered kings in some fashion, you need to look elsewhere. The Little Horn is likely a complete *unknown* at this moment.

## The Demon Beast

We have looked at the kingdom aspect of the Beast and the human aspect, but something very unusual is about to happen. The *demon aspect* of the Beast is about to come out of the *abyss*.

## The Beast From the Sea in Daniel 7

The demonic aspect of the Beast is about to *possess the human man* who is the king of the Beast Empire. Look at what Revelation says about this demon:

> *The Beast that you saw was, and is not, and is about to come up out of the abyss and go to destruction.* **(Rev 17:11)**

*He was* means that he existed on the earth at one time; and *but he is not* means that when John wrote Revelation in AD 90, the demon was already in the abyss. Then we have *and he will come up out of the abyss*, which means that he will come back in the future. This is all very strange and supernatural. Conservative scholars don't like this, but this is what the Bible says. And the Bible is *never* wrong.

It gets even stranger, as John continues about this demon:

> *They are seven kings; five have fallen, one is, the other has not yet come; and when he comes, he must remain a little while. The Beast which was and is not, is himself also an eighth and is one of the seven.* **(Rev 17:10-11)**

Here John tells us that there will be seven heads, and these seven heads are seven kings. As we now know, five have fallen or passed into history as of AD 90. One *is*, and that's the Roman Emperor — in AD 90, the Emperor was Domitian. The other head had not yet come.

Then John states something that is hard to comprehend: He says that the Beast which *was and is not* is himself an eighth and is also one of the seven. In other words, he will be one of the *original* kings. So, one of the kings is *going to come back*. But this king wasn't just any king. Either he was a demon, or he was a demon that possessed one of the kings. And we learn that he was in the abyss at that time (AD 90).

This is like a twisted riddle. So let's try to figure it out. You remember that we constructed a list of the seven kingdoms that make up the seven heads. Let's now try to put names to the kings of each of the kingdoms.

We already know the name of the sixth king, from the clues provided above — the Roman Emperor *Domitian*. He was ruling when John was given the prophecy. We can also fill in *Mohammed* for the Caliphate; *Alexander* for Greece; *Cyrus* for Persia, even though he was a relatively good king; *Nebuchadnezzar* for Babylon; and *Pharaoh* for Egypt. That's six of the seven heads.

Now let's try to figure out who was the ruler of *Assyria*. The Bible tells us directly who it was. The prophet Micah identifies Assyria with *Nimrod*:

> *They will shepherd the land of Assyria with the sword,*
> *The land of Nimrod at its entrances.* **(Mic 5:6)**

Who was Nimrod? He was the king of the whole earth who oversaw the building of the Tower of Babel right after the flood. So we will add Nimrod to our list — a most unusual king, to say the least.

Now that we've established our list of kings, let's look at the clues. We know that the final and eighth king, the Beast, was prior to John's day — *he was*. Unfortunately, this only eliminates two kings, Domitian and Mohammed. This leaves five earthly kings. Yet none were a demon or became a demon, as far as we know. So did a demon *possess* one or more of these five kings? Is that demon *coming back* in the future to possess the Little Horn? That will be our theory.

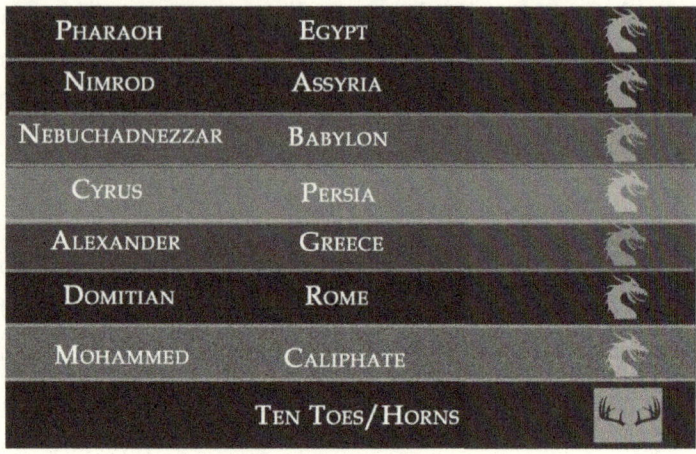

Figure 3-3

I suspect that it will be a single king from this list, one who *may have been possessed in the past.*

In the next article, we will demonstrate that the Little Horn will come out of the regions of either Greece, Turkey, Assyria, or northern Iraq. This revelation is based on our analysis of Dan 8. We recommend that you carefully consider that analysis and fully test it against your understanding of scripture when you reach that point in the book. But at this juncture, we ask that you passively accept our findings, so that we can continue our explanation here.

So, our theory is that the previous king that we're looking for will have come from the specific region which we have identified, a region which encompasses territories previously occupied by other kings on our list. That being the case, the king would have to be either *Alexander or Nimrod,* as these are the only two kings from this region.

As I stated earlier, Nimrod's name is found in an end times passage, something which I find quite interesting. The passage we previously looked at in Micah begins with this familiar verse about Jesus being born in Bethlehem:

> *But as for you, Bethlehem Ephrathah, too little to be among the clans of Judah, from you One will go forth for Me to be ruler in Israel. His goings forth are from long ago, From the days of eternity.* **(Mic 5:2)**

Then the passage transitions into end times territory. It claims that Jesus, born in Bethlehem, will be the peace, or *shalom,* of the Jewish people when someone known as *the Assyrian* invades their land and tramples on their Citadels — which likely includes the Holy Place or Temple:

> *Because at that time He will be great to the ends of the earth. This One will be our peace when the Assyrian invades our land, when he tramples on our citadels.* **(Mic 5:4-5)**

Who is this Assyrian? We aren't told, but as we've seen, the passage identifies the land with *Nimrod*. This doesn't prove that a demon possessed Nimrod and that it will return as a demonic spirit, but it makes me think that it might be.

The other candidate for the king who returns, *Alexander,* is never mentioned by name in the scriptures. That doesn't necessarily rule him out, but at least for now it makes him less attractive as a candidate.

So, let's look at Nimrod more closely and consider how his career might fit with the coming demon Beast. First, Nimrod was likely not his real name. In Hebrew, Nimrod literally means *the rebel*; and it was likely a derisive term used by Moses for this man who was the first true globalist. Nimrod attempted to set up a kingdom in opposition to the Lord.

Bible scholars have associated Nimrod with mythical characters like Gilgamesh, but rather than go to extremes chasing theories, even if there might be some truth in them, let's confine ourselves to what the Bible actually says:

> *He was a mighty hunter before the Lord therefore it is said like Nimrod a mighty hunter before the Lord.* **(Gen 10:9)**

This is a strange phrase. Why does it matter that Nimrod was a hunter, and why mention it twice?

Several of the Hebrew words used in this passage might help us to understand. Notice the word *before* in the phrase, *he was a mighty hunter before the Lord*. The word literally means *face*, as in *in your face*. It can be translated *in front of*, or *against*, or *in defiance of*. The correct translation then, according to the context, might be *he was a mighty hunter against the Lord*. That's why his name means *rebel*.

*Mighty hunter* is another very strange term. The Hebrew can also be translated as *mighty tyrant*. In the Old Testament, this word play is often used, and tyrants are referred to as hunters. So Nimrod might not just have been a king; he may have been a *tyrant king*.

Genesis continues:

> *The beginning of his kingdom was Babel and Erech and Accad and Calneh, in the land of Shinar. From that land he went forth into Assyria, and built Nineveh and Rehoboth-Ir and Calah, and Resen between Nineveh and Calah; that is the great city.* **(Gen 10:10-12)**

Notice the difference in the phrasing: Nimrod's kingdom started with the cities in the land of Shinar, which is Babylon. The difference in wording between Shinar and Assyria implies that Nimrod may not have *built* the Shinar cities. So it's possible that he *conquered* them instead. Nimrod was history's first globalist; and whether he was a conqueror or not, it appears that he may well have been a tyrant.

Josephus gives us a non-biblical, historical account of Nimrod. Speaking of the builders of Babel, he said:

> *Now it was Nimrod who excited them to such an affront and contempt of God. He was the grandson of Ham, the son of Noah. A bold man and of great strength of hand. He persuaded them not to ascribe it to God as if it were through his means they were happy, but to believe that it was their own courage which procured that happiness.* **(Josephus)**

This is supported by the biblical account of the building of the Tower of Babel:

> *Then they said come let us build for ourselves a city and a tower with its top in the heavens and let us make a name for ourselves.* **(Gen 11:4)**

## The Beast From the Sea in Daniel 7

So those building the tower were not seeking to glorify God's name but, rather, their own names and accomplishments. In response, God confused the languages of the people to end their unity. God does not destroy what is good, but what is evil. So we see that human globalism apart from God was what the spirit of that age was all about; and, frankly, it is what the spirit of our age is about, as well.

But was Nimrod *possessed*? And if he was, was the ancient spirit which possessed him the *same* one that will be coming to possess the man who will be the Beast? Let's see what we can determine.

In Isa 14, in a passage we traditionally use to refer to Satan, we read about the King of Babylon. The first king of this region, Babel, was Nimrod. Babel *was* Babylon:

> *How you have fallen from heaven, O star of the morning, son of the dawn! You have been cut down to the earth, you who have weakened the nations!* **(Isa 14:12)**

Notice that whoever this account is about fell from heaven. That means it *wasn't a man*. But it could have been Satan, or a fallen angel. Look at what the passage says next:

> *But you said in your heart, I will ascend to heaven; I will raise my throne above the stars of God, And I will sit on the mount of assembly. In the recesses of the north. I will ascend above the heights of the clouds; I will make myself like the Most High.* **(Isa 14:13-14)**

It speaks about ascending to heaven, raising a throne, and ascending above the clouds. Who tried to do these things?

*Nimrod*, when he tried to build a tower to reach to heaven. Look at the wording about the Tower of Babel again. It's the *same* concept:

> *Then they said come let us build for ourselves a city and a tower with its top in the heavens and let us make a name for ourselves.* **(Gen 11:4)**

Look again at the passage in Isa 14. Where does this demonic spirit attempt to make himself like the Most High? In the *recesses of the North*. Babel was considered the recesses of the north to Isaiah, who wrote the prophecy.

The passage in Isa 14 continues:

> *All the kings of the nations lie in glory, each in his own tomb. But you have been cast out of your tomb like a rejected branch.* **(Isa 14:18-19)**

This individual has been cast out of his tomb. Where was he cast? Could it be that he was a fallen angel and cast into the abyss? Certainly, this part of the passage cannot be speaking of Satan. So, it's my position that the passage is speaking of a *fallen angel*, the one that *possessed Nimrod,* and who was cast into the abyss.

The passage in Isa 14 concludes in this way:

> *They must not arise and take possession of the earth and fill the face of the world with cities.* **(Isa 14:21)**

Isn't that almost exactly what God feared would happen with the Tower of Babel?

## The Beast From the Sea in Daniel 7

Now, I know that you have always considered this passage in Isaiah to be about Satan. That's the traditional view. But do you see how the links with Nimrod, the demon that possessed him, and their globalist agenda are possibly a better match?

The Beast is *three things*: A kingdom, made out of seven heads which we've now identified; a man; and a demon. This *demon* possessed one of the first five kings, and the demon *comes back* out of the abyss. If we keep these things in mind, understanding the scripture in Daniel becomes much easier.

# Article Four

## Where Will the Little Horn Come From?

Very few questions are more important in eschatology than this one: Where will the Antichrist come from? I'm sure some ideas flashed into your mind immediately. There are those who believe the USA is a possible source. Some think Israel. Others consider Rome likely. Or perhaps someplace in the European Union. Still others think Russia will produce the Antichrist. There are so many theories, so many powerful and selfish men to choose from!

But how many of you guessed the *location given in Dan 8*, from the prophecy of the Ram and the Goat? Did anybody choose the region of Turkey?

Dan 8 is not a prominent prophecy, so many of you are probably not familiar with it. The rest are probably thinking that prophecy was fulfilled long ago, by Alexander the Great. Frankly, I used to think that way myself, just seven or eight years ago. Then I ran into these verses in the middle Dan 8:

> *"The vision pertains to the time of the end"* ... He said, *"Behold, I am going to let you know what will occur at the final period of the indignation, for it pertains to the appointed time of the end."* **(Dan 8:17, 19)**

These are the words of the angel Gabriel, who's showing Daniel this vision of the future. Gabriel tells him *three times* that this vision pertains to the time of the end, or the end times. He didn't tell him just one time, but three times. As we mentioned in Article One, there are no explanation marks in Hebrew. If

## Where Will the Little Horn Come From?

Gabriel mentioned it three times, then we know that this is *important information*.

That repetition caught my attention. Hopefully it has now caught yours, as well. Perhaps Gabriel knew that he really had to emphasize the point in order for us to fully grasp that Dan 8 has future implications.

Traditionally, the first part of Dan 8 has been considered a prophecy that was fulfilled completely in the past, with no application to the future. If you *Google* Dan 8, practically every commentary you read prior to 2010 will state that the first portion of the prophecy was fulfilled by Alexander the Great, and that his empire was subsequently divided among his generals. All of which took place hundreds of years before Jesus.

But the words of Gabriel quoted above changed my way of thinking about prophecy. I realized that a single prophecy might have a *first, partial fulfillment in the past,* close to the time when it was given, like that of Alexander the Great, and then a *second, final fulfillment in the future.* This is frequently referred to as *near/far fulfillment*.

This prophecy mentions the Little Horn, the Antichrist, and the region where he comes from. So it is *not* a trivial prophecy at all. Additionally, as we mentioned in Article One, it seems to mark the beginning of the end times. For both of these reasons, we should pay special attention to it.

### History or Future?

Those who believe that the events which took place between Persia and Greece some 2,300 years ago fulfilled the prophecy typically believe that the prophecy was *completely* fulfilled at that time. They believe there is no *future* component to the prophecy. But 10 years ago, religious teacher and author Mark Davidson noticed the Dan 8 passage and wrote about it in his book entitled *Daniel Revisited* (2013). There is no escaping the truth of God's Word. When I saw the passage with fresh eyes in Davidson's book, I realized that the vision pertains to the time of the end. This passage hit me like a sledgehammer. It was like my eyes were *unsealed*.

So I immediately set about seeking answers to the question of whether Alexander the Great fulfilled the prophecy perfectly, or whether he had done so only partially. This was my first step toward understanding the prophecy. Dan 8 tells us that the *prominent horn*, which most think was *Alexander*, will be the first king of his empire:

> *The shaggy Goat represents the kingdom of Greece, and the large horn that is between his eyes is the **first** king.*
> **(Dan 8:21)**

However, we know from history that Alexander's title was Alexander III of Macedon. He *wasn't* the first king of his kingdom; he wasn't even the first Alexander. In fact, although history is not exactly clear, he appears to have been the 23rd king of Macedon. Already we have a *problem* with a perfect historic fulfillment.

The prophecy goes on to tell us that the first king will die, and his empire will be split into four sub-kingdoms. At first, this seems like a match with Alexander. Alexander *did* die suddenly, and his empire *was* divided among his generals. Historically, this is known as the *Wars of the Diadochi*, a string of wars fought over a 40-year period which resulted in the empire being

## Where Will the Little Horn Come From?

divided into some *two dozen* separate entities. Then, as warfare took its toll, the numbers of surviving generals and territorial divisions decreased until, eventually, the former Macedonian Empire was consolidated into *five* separate kingdoms, which were further consolidated into three with just *two prominent ones*: The *Seleucids* and the *Ptolemys*. But here's the important point — there was *never* a time when there were *four* distinct sub-kingdoms for any significant period of time, as scripture seems to indicate.

So why is the internet full of maps of four divisions? In my opinion, there will always be those who attempt to re-shape history to match their notion of prophecy. What I find fascinating is that the biblical articles cannot even agree with themselves over which of the Diadochi were the four divisions. Some claim one group of four, while others claim a separate group of kingdoms!

In conclusion, Alexander's empire was certainly not *initially* divided into four separate kingdoms; and it *never* settled into *four* distinct entities. This is another incredible problem for the historic fulfillment of this prophecy.

The prophecy then moves on to someone it calls the Little Horn. Those who subscribe to a historic interpretation of the prophecy assume this refers to a man named Antiochus Epiphanes, a king from the Seleucid Empire who persecuted the Jews and desecrated the Temple in Jerusalem. This was a very bad man, and he is probably the Bible's best foreshadowing of the coming Antichrist.

However, there are several things in the text that just can't apply to Antiochus alone. The text says he caused some of the host and some of the stars of heaven (meaning angels) to fall to the earth. *No one* believes he actually did this:

> *It grew up to the host of heaven and caused some of the host and some of the stars to fall to the earth, and it trampled them down. It even magnified itself to be equal with the Commander of the host.* **(Dan 8:10-11)**

Additionally, as we see, he magnified himself to be equal with Jesus, the Commander of the Host.

Historicists claim this Commander is God the Father. However, the Hebrew word translated *commander* is *sar*, meaning *prince*. Certainly, God the Father isn't considered the prince. This is *Jesus*, who wasn't born for another 160 years.

Later, in the same passage, the prophecy states that the Little Horn will destroy mighty men and the holy people. Now, Antiochus did persecute the Jews; but he was rather ineffective as a military commander. He never conquered the Egyptians, whom he repeatedly attacked; and he even backed down and turned away when confronted by the Romans.

The prophecy also states that the Little Horn will be broken without human agency, but that isn't true of Antiochus either. He was defeated by the Maccabees. The Jewish celebration of *Hanukkah* annually remembers the rededication of the Temple following this victory.

Finally, the prophecy also tells us that the Little Horn will arise when the rulers of the four kingdoms into which the Goat is split reach their end. However, historically this is also not a match. Antiochus reigned around 160 BC, but the Diadochi continued their reign for another hundred years, until the Romans finally acquired the territory.

In conclusion, there are at least *seven inconsistencies* with an historic fulfillment of this prophecy. When we add the three pronouncements by the angel Gabriel that the prophecy is for the *end times*, I think we need to lay aside any previous notions that this was a one-and-done prophecy, fulfilled completely in the past. I believe that there is a coming *future fulfillment*, as well.

I realize this may be shocking to you. It certainly was to me! If you need to, please reread this section and then verify the historic facts that have been presented.

## Future Fulfillment

We are now certain that the Dan 8 prophecy is not one which we should just pass over and ignore because we think it was fulfilled long ago. It wasn't. It applies to the *future*, and we need to examine further how it might be fulfilled. It might be something that will happen next week, next year, or sometime in the next decade — or beyond. Every Christian needs to know about this prophecy and consider its implications, especially those concerning the origins of the Antichrist.

Dan 8 begins with Daniel seeing a vision of a *Ram* with *two horns*. We are told later in the prophecy that this Ram represents the Kings of Media and Persia. This is yet another thing that throws everyone off and makes them believe the prophecy has *only* a historic fulfillment. Clearly, Persia was an ancient country.

Today the country of Iran occupies the same piece of land represented by ancient Persia. But imagine how confused Daniel would have been if Gabriel had told him that the Ram represented the Kings of *Iran*. He'd wonder where that was! That is why all ancient prophecies use the names of the countries and land masses as they existed *at that time*. The prophecy of the Gog-Magog War is another example of a prophecy that contains the names of ancient kingdoms. And yet 99% of scholars still believe this prophecy from Ezekiel will only have a *future* fulfillment:

> *I am against you, O Gog, prince of Rosh, Meshech and Tubal. I will turn you about and put hooks into your jaws, and I will bring you out, and all your army, horses and horsemen, all of them splendidly attired, a great company with buckler and shield, all of them wielding swords; Persia, Ethiopia and Put with them, all of them with shield and helmet; Gomer with all its troops; Beth-Togarmah from the remote parts of the north.* **(Ezek 38:3-6)**

Just as in Dan 8, Persia is mentioned in this prophecy, along with a host of other ancient kingdoms. But, as we stated, no one believes Ezek 38 is a fulfilled prophecy. Scholars all accept that *Persia* in these verses refers to modern *Iran*. Therefore, we should not hesitate for a moment to consider that the Ram of Dan 8 is modern Iran, especially since we are told directly that this vision applies to the time of the end.

## The War Between the Ram and Goat

Rams are known for head-butting, and that is exactly what the text tells us will happen:

## Where Will the Little Horn Come From?

> *I saw the Ram butting westward, northward, and southward, and no other Beasts could stand before him nor was there anyone to rescue from his power, but he did as he pleased and magnified himself.* **(Dan 8:4)**

The prophecy suggests that the nation of Iran will expand, butting its way west, north, and southward. We are told this head-butting begins in the ancient Persian city of Susa. A westward advance would put Iran into Syria, Lebanon, and Gaza. And guess what? Iran already has controlling interests in two of these areas, and it's a major player in Syria, as well. North of Susa is northern Iraq, where Iran already has influence. And to the south is Yemen. Iran also has influence there with the Houthis. And just like the prophecy indicates, *no other nation has interfered with Iran's expansion*. No one has been strong enough in the Middle East *to rescue from his power*.

Has this portion of the prophecy been fulfilled? Maybe. Iran has certainly butted its influence into all of the directions mentioned in Dan 8. It is also possible that this prophecy has begun, but perhaps is not yet complete. Maybe Iran will expand further still, using military or non-military means — or both.

*I strongly believe that the prophecy has begun.* If this is true, then we are, by definition, in the end times — because Dan 8:17 tells us that the prophecy relates to the time of the end. This means we have reached that point in time when the book of Daniel was intended by God to be unsealed (Dan 12:4). Make no mistake: In my opinion, *we are in the end times!*

In Article One, we indicated a possible date of 1980 for the start of the end times. This isn't a date we picked out of a hat. It is the approximate start of the Ram's head-butting to the west, north, and south. The Iranian Revolution took place in 1978. And soon after, they began to wield their influence in other Shia Muslim countries.

Joel Richardson wrote his landmark book, *Antichrist: Islam's Awaited Messiah* (later retitled *Islamic Antichrist*) in 2006. This marked, in my opinion, the literary beginning of the unsealing of Daniel. So somewhere in the 25 years between these two dates, 1980 and 2006, the symbolic jar was broken in heaven and the Holy Spirit began to teach us what the book of Daniel means.

## The Prophecy Continues

Let's continue to examine the rest of the prophecy. We are next told that the Ram *magnifies itself*. Some translations say it *becomes great*. What might that mean? Iranians are predominantly Shia Muslims and are *twelvers*. This means that they are awaiting their Messiah, the 12th Imam, who supposedly is in hiding while waiting to be revealed. Iranian leaders say they already know who he is. Might he be revealed during this period of Iranian expansion? Perhaps. That is my theory, that the *revealing of the 12th Imam* is how Iran magnifies itself.

Then, according to the prophecy, the tables turn. Daniel saw a *Goat* coming from the West with a single, prominent horn:

> *A male Goat was coming from the west over the surface of the whole earth without touching the ground; and the Goat had a conspicuous horn between his eyes.* **(Dan 8:5)**

Later in the prophecy, this Goat is identified as the nation of *Yavan*. Our English Bibles translate this nation as Greece, but

## Where Will the Little Horn Come From?

Yavan is correct. Yavan is another ancient nation and was located along the borders of eastern Greece and western Turkey. It is the area surrounding the Bosporus straits, and the most prominent city in this region is Istanbul, the former capital of the Ottoman Empire. Let's keep that in mind. There is no current nation in this location. The biblical nation is a combination of two current nations, Greece and Turkey. In my opinion, this represents a nation that *will* form in the near future, perhaps a revived Ottoman Empire. The Ottoman capital was Istanbul, so that makes sense.

We're told in the prophecy that the *Goat attacks the Ram* and hurls him to the ground:

> *He came up to the Ram that had the two horns, which I had seen standing in front of the canal, and rushed at him in his mighty wrath. I saw him come beside the Ram, and he was enraged at him; and he struck the Ram and shattered his two horns, and the Ram had no strength to withstand him. So he hurled him to the ground and trampled on him.* **(Dan 8:6-7)**

The interesting word in this passage is *enraged*. Yavan, or what we've been assuming is the revived Ottoman Empire, is enraged with Iran. Why? What could make this new nation so angry with Iran that it attacks its Shiite Muslim neighbor, knowing that the superpowers of the world will strongly disapprove?

We will discuss this further in future articles, but could it be that Iran declaring that the Muslim Messiah is Shia, and not Sunni, will be the breaking point of their current co-existence? I think this is the most likely reason.

The religious divide between Shia Iran and Sunni nations goes back many years, to the first years after the death of Mohammed. *Sunni* Muslims are found in Turkey and Saudi Arabia and make up about 85% of Islam. *Shiite* Muslims make up the remaining 15% and are largely based in Iran. The two groups are struggling to define *true Islam*. You can imagine the hostility that would arise in Sunni nations if Iran were to declare that their Messiah has come — and it turns out that he is Shia, not Sunni.

According to the prophecy, we know that *Yavan* wins and Iran is crushed, just as the foreshadowing of Alexander the Great crushed Persia. It is at this point that Yavan magnifies itself, just as Iran had previously. But the Bible adds a word here; it says the Goat (Yavan) magnifies itself *exceedingly*.

Does the revived Ottoman Empire, now based in Istanbul, declare itself to be a Caliphate, a worldwide Islamic government? I think that is the most likely scenario. This would scare the world to death: Imagine 1.3 billion Muslims united under one ruler — that's a possible doomsday scenario!

We don't know how the world will ultimately respond to the *magnification* of Yavan. But God's Word tells us that Yavan's first king is *broken*:

> *Then the male goat magnified himself exceedingly. But as soon as he was mighty, the large horn was broken; and in its place there came up four conspicuous horns toward the four winds of heaven.* **(Dan 8:8)**

This may mean that the first king is killed and the empire is broken into four sub-kingdoms. In my opinion, this sounds

## Where Will the Little Horn Come From?

like the world superpowers forcibly dismantle the Caliphate before it can get organized, similar in fashion to what happened when Germany was broken into pieces following World War II. In any case, we see in the pages of the prophecy that this Caliphate will be broken into four segments, aligned with the four winds — north, south, east, and west.

We now come to the main point of this article, which is the rising of the Little Horn, the *Antichrist*. We are told that he *arises* out of one of the four horns, or sub-kingdoms, of the Goat.

> *Out of one of them came forth a rather small horn which grew exceedingly great toward the south, toward the east, and toward the Beautiful Land.* **(Dan 8:9)**

This would mean, of course, that the Antichrist is from the *Middle East*. And in my humble opinion, this is the real reason that most scholars refuse to accept Dan 8 as future prophecy — because it identifies the part of the world from which the Antichrist arises, and they don't like what it says. It disrupts the *Euro-centric* view most have of the end times.

Amazingly, this verse gives us a more specific prophecy about which of the four divisions the Antichrist comes from. We're told the power of the Antichrist increases to the south, to the east, and to the west, toward the beautiful land, which is Israel. Why doesn't the power of the Antichrist increase to the *north*? It can mean that the Antichrist comes from the *northernmost* of the four kingdoms, which would be the most northern division of the newly re-formed *Ottoman Caliphate*.

No matter what you think about Obama or Trump or the next American president, the Antichrist isn't American. No matter what you think about the pope or the European Union, the Antichrist isn't from a revived Roman Empire. Dan 8 tells us he is *Middle Eastern*! This is an *extremely important understanding*.

## Applications

While you contemplate this sobering revelation, I have several recommendations for how we can best apply this prophecy:

- We need to stop exclusively looking for the Antichrist in America, Europe, and other places that clearly do not align with prophecy. If we don't, we may miss the true Antichrist, who, according to prophecy, will almost certainly be Middle Eastern.

- The Antichrist arises only after the Goat is divided into four sub-kingdoms. So, we should stop looking for him now, and patiently wait for the signs given us in the Bible.

- Knowing what events take place in the near future is important. We can apply that knowledge for Kingdom purposes in something I term *apocalyptic evangelism*, which means seeing something in the world that was prophesied, and then testifying that the event is found in the Bible.

The coming great war between Yavan and Iran is one of those events that every Christian should be watching for. When we see this war happen, and when we witness Iran being crushed, Christians need to share Dan 8 and its prophecies with every person they know, for two reasons:

### Where Will the Little Horn Come From?

*First*, it will represent perhaps one of the strongest apologetic arguments of all time, an undeniable *prophecy-fulfilled* before the eyes of the world.

*Second*, Christians in particular need to understand what the prophecy says will happen from that point on, that the revised Ottoman Empire that forms and crushes Iran isn't the Beast Empire, and its leader won't be the Antichrist. It will be so tempting to think that it is.

I personally think this is part of the deception that Jesus warned us is coming. There will be many false messiahs making the real one more difficult to recognize. We need to keep our eyes on someone coming out of the northern division of the Goat empire. That is the region from which the Antichrist will come, according to Dan 8.

# Article Five

## The Four Beasts Are the Four Horns

Dan 7 opens with what may be the four most bizarre creatures of all time: Four Beasts, some with wings, and some with multiple heads. In this article, we will explore what they might be and when they might come upon the world.

In Articles Three and Four we discussed the main points of Dan 7 and Dan 8. Article Three examined the fourth of these Beasts in detail, what is universally known as the *terrifying* Beast. We learned that the Beast has *three natures*: It's a kingdom, a king, and a demon, all rolled into one. In Article Four, we discussed the events that precede the coming of the king aspect of the Beast, and what part of the world he comes from.

These two articles probably seemed very different to you, but they actually have several similarities. In fact, it is likely they are describing many of the same events. The night vision Daniel received in Dan 7 left him sick, and he didn't understand it. Just two years later, a second vision was given to Daniel to assist him in understanding his previous vision.

> *In the third year of the reign of Belshazzar the king a vision appeared to me, Daniel, subsequent to the one which appeared to me previously.* **(Dan 8:1)**

The Hebrew word translated as *subsequent* in this verse is *achar*, which literally means *hindquarters*. This can simply mean *after*, but it can also mean the *second or back half*, as in the second part of the first vision. Since Daniel gave us the dates of both visions, it would be redundant to say that this second vision is the one that came after the first. More likely, Daniel is telling us that the two visions are related and that the *second vision* in Dan 8 *explains the first* vision in Dan 7. At least that's our working theory.

The similarities between the two visions seem to confirm our position. In both visions we learn about the four winds of heaven. These four winds are instrumental to the appearance of the four kingdoms. After the four kingdoms arise, the Little Horn comes up out of a group of horns — 10 horns in Dan 7, and four horns in Dan 8.

Given the similarities between the two chapters in Daniel and their prophecies, we will begin our study in this article with the assumption that Dan 8 is an explanation of the same events taking place in Dan 7. That would mean that both chapters are about the *same four kingdoms*.

## The Four Beasts

In Dan 7, the four kingdoms *are* called the four Beasts:

> *The fourth Beast will be a fourth kingdom on the earth, which will be different from all the other kingdoms.* **(Dan 7:23)**

> *These great Beasts, which are four in number, are four kings who will arise from the earth.* **(Dan 7:17)**

And we see from these verses that the four Beasts are *both* four kingdoms and four kings that arise on the earth.

Now, we have previously learned that the four winds of heaven are angels and that they stir up the Great Sea, which we established symbolically represents the Gentile nations. We also learned that the Great Sea is the eastern Mediterranean Sea. So the four Beasts come out of the Gentile nations in that region. Putting it all together, we find that the Beasts arise because the four winds of heaven are causing a great commotion by *stirring up* the sea. We will soon determine what this commotion is.

The four winds of heaven from Dan 7 are mentioned in other places in Daniel and by other prophets. As we know, they are seen again in Dan 8 in relation to the formation of four kingdoms, or horns. Then they are seen again in Dan 11, where we once again see these same four winds dividing an existing kingdom into four new kingdoms.

The time period represented by these prophecies will be a time of great *commotion* among the nations of the earth and will include the breakup, possibly forced, of the great kingdom of the Goat (Yavan) into four smaller kingdoms. Our theory is that although each of the *prophecies* in Daniel seem to discuss different events and people, they are *all related* to the same four Beasts and the same formation of the four horns of the Goat.

There are additional references to the four winds in Jeremiah, Zechariah, Matthew, and Mark. And all of these references are in an end times setting. Are they all in some way related to the four Beasts? Perhaps.

## The First Three Beasts are Future

Before we get too far ahead of ourselves, let's focus first on the first three Beasts, which have been described for us as being like-a-Lion with Eagle's wings; like-a-Bear; and like-a-Leopard with four heads and four wings.

## The Four Beasts Are the Four Horns

About which you may be thinking, "I already know that these Beasts represent the historic kingdoms of Babylon, Persia, and Greece; and they are the same as the first three metals found in Nebuchadnezzar's statue." I'd like you to consider the possibility that maybe they aren't, although the Beasts and the statue are very similar.

There are *four reasons* they may not be exactly the same. *First*, let's look at a verse we examined earlier in this article.

> *These great Beasts which are four in number are four kings who will arise from the earth.* (**Dan 7:17**)

One key to understanding this passage may be that it says the Beasts *will arise*. This implies that they'll arise at some time in the future. When Daniel received this vision in the first year of King Belshazzar, Nebuchadnezzar had been dead for 10 years. So this verse cannot be speaking of him or ancient Babylon. They had already arisen at this point.

The *second* reason that the Beasts and the statue may not be the same is that in Nebuchadnezzar's dream of the statue, all of the kingdoms were destroyed *at the same time*, when the stone smashed into the statue.

> *Then the iron the clay the bronze the silver and the gold all together were broken in pieces and became like chaff of the summer threshing floors.* (**Dan 2:35**)

But in Dan 7, the first three Beasts were allowed to live on for some time *after* the destruction of the fourth Beast.

> *As I looked, the Beast was killed, and its body destroyed and given over to be burned with fire. As for the rest of the Beasts, their dominion was taken away, but their*

*lives were prolonged for a season and a time.* **(Dan 7:11-12)**

This is a *significant* difference. The four kingdoms cannot be both *destroyed* at the same time and *not destroyed* at the same time. If you thought the statue and the Beasts were the same, this single difference proves that they are not. But there are two additional reasons why they are different.

The *third* reason is that on Nebuchadnezzar's statue, the 10 toes are a *separate* section: They are part of the end times manifestation of the iron kingdom when it becomes iron and clay mixed. The legs start out as iron and *transition* into the toes. The toes are separate from the legs of iron, the fourth kingdom of the statue. But when the fourth Beast appears in Dan 7, it *already* has the 10 horns, so it is already an end times manifestation when it *first* appears.

*Fourth* and finally, as we have already discovered, the Greek Empire was never divided into four kingdoms, but, rather, was broken into several dozen, before eventually coalescing into just three kingdoms. But it was *never* four kingdoms for any significant period of time. Yet we see that the *third Beast* in Dan 7, the Leopard, has *four* heads and four wings. This does not compare with the historic Greece that never was divided into *four* nations.

So, for these reasons, we believe that the four Beasts are future, end times manifestations. I know this is a shock to the majority of our readers, but that is what the scriptures seem to imply.

# The Four Beasts Are the Four Horns

## Who Are the First Three Beasts?

If that is so, then who are the first three Beasts? Some who realize that they represent future kingdoms look at the names of the Beasts and attempt to apply modern nationalities. When they hear *Lion*, they think England. Some hear *Eagle's wings*, and think America. Others think the *Bear* is a good fit for Russia. But, of course, this is not a particularly valid method of interpreting scripture. Throughout history there have been dozens of nations associated with Lions, and Eagles, and Bears. Oh, my!

We have already seen that the Beasts come out of the eastern part of the Mediterranean Sea, and none of the above nations do. We need to see what the Bible tells us about what these names might mean and what nations might be associated with them.

As we've mentioned before, there are great similarities between the statue's kingdoms of gold, silver, and, bronze, and what we are told about the Lion, the Bear, and the Leopard. Let's look more closely at those similarities. Perhaps our study will give us a clue as to who these future nations might be.

The Lion with Eagle's wings sure sounds like Nebuchadnezzar's Babylon. Babylon was even called a *Lion* in Jer 4:7. In Jer 4:13, the king's military and horses were compared to *Eagles*.

We also learn that this Beast has his *Beast mind* taken away, to be replaced with a *man's mind*. This is similar to Dan 4, where we saw that Nebuchadnezzar's pride led him to be punished by God: For seven years the king was mad, living and acting like a Beast, until he repented and his man's mind was restored to him.

Yes, these things related to Babylon and Nebuchadnezzar seem incredibly similar to what we read about the *Lion with Eagle's wings*. If we hadn't just proven that the Beasts are end times related, we might be inclined to believe that this prophecy was about Babylon.

In the prophecy, The *Bear* is lifted up on one side. Since we know the bear has two sides, by inference the *lifting* may mean that it is a divided kingdom, with one side being stronger (higher) than the other. For those still stuck on the association of the Bear and Russia, this is actually another reason why it can't be Russia: Russia is not a divided nation, nor does it have a stronger side and a weaker side. But the ancient Medo-Persian Empire was a joint kingdom just like that. So this Beast actually resembles that ancient kingdom. But that, too, is in the past.

The *Leopard* is given dominion in Dan 7. This is a parallel to the *bronze* kingdom of the statue ruling the whole earth in Dan 2.

And the fourth, *terrifying Beast* of Dan 7 has *teeth of iron*, just like the fourth kingdom of the *statue is iron*. The fourth Beast also *crushes and tramples* with its feet, just as the fourth kingdom crushes and pulverizes the kingdoms that went before it.

Finally, the kingdoms of the statue are presented in the *exact same order* as the four Beasts; the one *like* Babylon first, the one *like* Persia second, and the one *like* Greece third.

I think the last paragraph is a *key* to our understanding, and I believe that the word *"like"* is *extremely important* in this passage. It's a little word most scholars have overlooked. If Babylon is the Lion with Eagle's wings then the first Beast is *like* it. Like it, but not exactly the same. If the Bear is Persia, then the second Beast is *like* it, but not exactly the same. And so on.

## The Four Beasts Are the Four Horns

This *radically new viewpoint* reinforces what we've been saying about the four Beasts being end times manifestations of the earlier kingdoms. The first Beast is *like Babylon*; the second is *like Persia*; and the third is *like Greece*. How exactly are they *like* these previous empires? That is what we need to determine.

Might they exist on the same approximate piece of land? That seems highly likely. For instance, might the first Beast like-a-Lion exist on the land that was once Babylon? Or the second Beast that is like-a-Bear exist on the land that was once Persia? And the third Beast that is like-a-Leopard on territory that was once the Hellenistic Greek Empire? We aren't told this directly, but this is a definite possibility.

Is it possible that these Beasts exhibit other qualities similar to their ancient counterparts? If so, it is likely that they will exhibit traits that are listed in the text of the scripture — meaning they will be *like* the former empires based on overwhelming *character traits* referenced in Dan 7.

We see from Dan 7 that the first Beast that is *like-a-Lion* was made to stand up on its feet and was given the mind of a man. Let's see what we might learn from ancient Babylon about this character trait of the first Beast.

Nebuchadnezzar's loss of status and casting out to become a Beast is recorded in Dan 4, where we learn that for the sin of pride, Nebuchadnezzar spent seven years as a Beast. Every student of prophecy should be picking up their ears at that statement. They should recognize the similarity between this 7-year period and Daniel's 70th Week, which was also a 7-year period. Will the first Beast like-a-Lion become a Beast for that exact period, the 70th Week of Daniel, only to be raised up on its feet and given a man's civilized mind at the end?

We are told that after the destruction of the fourth terrifying Beast, the first Beast is allowed to *live on*. Will the first Beast *like-a-Lion* only be a Beast for a *temporary* period of time? Does it start out with a civilized mind, become a Beast for the 70th Week of Daniel, and then become civilized once again at the end? That would be my best guess.

About the second Beast, the one that is *like-a-Bear*, we learn three facts. First, it is raised up on one side. Second, it has three ribs in its mouth. And third, it is told to consume much flesh. As we previously mentioned, being raised up implies that there are two sides to this kingdom and that one is stronger than the other. The three ribs may mean that it consumes three other small nations. And the *consuming much flesh* may well imply that it has an appetite for conquest. Later in this book, we will discuss what this might actually look like in future world events.

The third Beast — which is like-*a-Leopard* — has four heads and it is the only one of the Beasts that is said to be given dominion. Might it consume the other three Beasts by proxy, giving it total control? We will discuss that aspect in the very next article.

After the first three Beasts have made their appearance, we are introduced to the fourth, *terrifying Beast*, the one with 10 horns:

> *After this I kept looking in the night visions, and behold, a fourth Beast, dreadful and terrifying and extremely strong; and it had large iron teeth. It devoured and crushed and trampled down the remainder with its feet; and it was different from all the Beasts that were before it, and it had ten horns.* **(Dan 7:7)**

## The Four Beasts Are the Four Horns

The mouth, feet, and horns of this fourth Beast are its identifying features. We know from Rev 13 that the fourth Beast has the *mouth of a Lion*, and that's where the teeth are, the *iron teeth*.

> *For a nation has come up against my land powerful and beyond number its teeth are Lion's teeth and it has the fangs of a Lioness.* **(Joel 1:6)**

The fourth Beast also has the *feet of a Bear*, and these feet trample what the mouth doesn't consume. Lastly, the *claws* of the Beast are made from the *bronze* of the Greek Empire. So the strength of the fourth and final Beast comes from these three, constituent parts of its empire. Consider if you will that these elements may be focused on Israel:

> *When they (Israel) had grazed, they became full, they were filled, and their heart was lifted up; therefore, they forgot me. So, I am to them like a Lion; like a Leopard I will lurk beside the way. I will fall upon them like a Bear robbed of her cubs.* **(Hosea 13:6-8)**

Look closely: We see judgment like-a-Lion, like-a-Bear, and like-a-Leopard falling upon Israel.

Let's take a moment to review what we've uncovered so far. The winds of heaven will stir up the Gentile nations to bring forth these four end times kingdoms. We gave four reasons that they will be end times kingdoms and not Babylon, Persia, and Greece. These end times kingdoms will be *like* the ancient kingdoms of Nebuchadnezzar's statue in several important ways, which may include their geographical footprint and certain other characteristics.

## Comparing Dan 7 and Dan 8

Now that we understand these things, let's apply them by figuring out the order of end times events. The key to this ordering of events is the very next chapter, Dan 8, which is the vision given to Daniel to help him understand the vision in Dan 7.

As we mentioned at the beginning of this article, Dan 7 and Dan 8 share many common elements: The Little Horn, four kingdoms, the winds of heaven, and in this case, references that they are both related to the future. In Dan 8, this reference is found in the three direct pronouncements of the angel. In Dan 7, it is implied, as we just learned.

From the previous article we know that Dan 8 begins with two new and very *different animals*, a *Ram* and a *Goat*. The vast majority of the Church assumes that these two animals are the same as two of the four Beasts, namely the Bear and the Leopard, and that they are also the same as two of the four kingdoms of Nebuchadnezzar's statute, specifically, Persia and Greece.

But think about that for a moment: If God's purpose of this vision in Dan 8 is to *clarify* the four Beasts and the rest of Dan 7, adding two more symbols, two different animals, certainly does not make things clearer. It makes things *more complex*.

You might also wonder where the other two Beasts are, the one like-a-Lion that starts things off and the most important one, the fourth, terrifying Beast. It makes no sense to leave them out of the explanation. That certainly doesn't help with clarification either.

## The Four Beasts Are the Four Horns

For things to make sense, these two new animals, the Ram and the Goat, must be *different* from the four Beasts of Dan 7. In fact, in my opinion, they are the *precursors* of the four Beasts.

The vision in Dan 8 was given to Daniel by the angel Gabriel. And based on the material in that second vision, we can surmise that its purpose was to provide answers to *four important questions*:

1. When do the four Beasts emerge?

2. What events take place before the four Beasts arise?

3. Where exactly does the Little Horn come from?

4. What takes place after the Little Horn arises?

Let's look at these questions one at a time.

With respect to the *first* question, in our analysis of Dan 7 we concluded that there were *four reasons* why the prophecy was not yet fulfilled, why it is an *end times* prophecy. This analysis required a certain amount of deduction on our part. However, we see in Dan 8 that it appears that God didn't want to leave such things to chance. He wanted to make things perfectly clear. So He communicated the details in plain language via His angel. In fact, someone in the appearance of a man (probably Jesus, Himself) commands Gabriel to *make Daniel understand*.

> *Gabriel make this man understand the vision.* **(Dan 8:17)**

Gabriel then proceeds to tell Daniel *three times* in clear language — not in images or symbols — that the vision of the Ram and the Goat is about the *end times*, the final indignation, and the appointed time of the end. What could be clearer? Yet, as you know, this is far from clear to most Christians, even today, because the book of Daniel has been supernaturally sealed.

Let's look at the *second* question: What events occur prior to the four Beasts coming up out of the sea? We have already surmised that the Ram and the Goat are the precursor nations to the four Beasts. They come before the Beasts, and the wars between the nations represented by these animals are the events that precede the appearing of the four Beasts.

As to the *third* question regarding the origins of the four Beasts, the angel Gabriel was very specific about the identity of the precursor nations. Daniel was made to know precisely where the four Beasts would come from. If Gabriel hadn't given Daniel this information, it might have been assumed that the four Beasts could come from anywhere — even Canada, or Bolivia. But that wasn't the case. Gabriel told Daniel directly that the *Ram* was the kings of the Medes and the Persians, whose territory existed essentially where Iran is located today. And Daniel was made to understand that the *Goat* is Yavan, which is the area occupied by Greece and western Turkey today. Gabriel wanted Daniel to understand that this is a *Middle Eastern* prophecy.

The *fourth* question concerning the things that take place after Little Horn arises is a little more difficult to answer. Prior to him arising, the Goat has a single prominent horn. It is a single kingdom with a single leader. Scripture tells us that this Goat kingdom becomes exceedingly great. What would happen in today's world if a Middle Eastern power overcame Iran and became exceedingly great? I think a fair assumption is that the world's super-powers or the UN would break it up. That is,

## The Four Beasts Are the Four Horns

exactly what we are told will happen according to scripture. The Goat kingdom will be broken up into four smaller, weaker kingdoms; into four horns.

In my opinion, this is the point in the story where the four Beasts enter. I believe the four Beasts are the four horns of the Goat. Scripture interprets scripture:

- *First*, each of the *four groups* relate to a kingdom, a horn, and a Beast.

- *Second*, the four horns come up toward the *four winds of heaven*, just as the four Beasts come out of the sea after it is stirred up by these same winds.

- *Third*, in my opinion, this *stirring up* of the sea is the war between the Ram and the Goat, which is then followed by the *breakup* of the Goat kingdom.

- *Fourth*, arising from one of the horns comes the Little Horn. In Dan 7, we learn that the Little Horn comes up from among the 10 horns. This *coming up* of the Little Horn occurs at the same place in the account — after the formation of the four kingdoms (horns or Beasts).

- *Fifth*, if we accept that the four horns of the Goat are *four of the 10 horns* we read about in Dan. 7, per my theory, then we have an additional similarity. In fact, all 10 horns might be created at this exact same time as the four horns of the Goat.

- *Sixth* and finally, we see that the exact same process occurs in Dan 8 as in Dan 7. In Dan 7, the Little Horn *plucks out* three of the original horns by the roots. In Dan 8 we read that Little Horn became great towards three directions of the compass — to the south, east and west. This becoming great in three directions is the *same process* as plucking out three horns.

These, then, are *six separate reasons* why the four Beasts of Dan 7 are the four horns of Dan 8. Why has no one seen this before?

Well, actually, someone has. We have developed an interactive community on my YouTube channel (see link in the opening pages of this book). One of the brilliant commentators there was the first person I know of to make this connection. What I have written here is primarily the result of further research based on her findings.

Clearly, the book of Daniel is no longer sealed. *Many are going back and forth*, as it says in Dan 12:4. And knowledge is increasing. The jar is broken open, and the Holy Spirit is enabling all of us to see the truth laid out in the scroll of Daniel. We just have to open our eyes to see.

# Article Six

## The Rise of the Little Horn

Scripture provides us with a clear picture of the rise of the Little Horn. It is detailed in Dan 7 and 8. The Beast, the Man of Sin, the Antichrist, the Assyrian, the King of Babylon are all titles that scripture applies to this Little Horn of Daniel. In this article we're going to look at *explosive new information* regarding the beginnings of Little Horn, the nations that might make up the 10 horns of the Beast, and the nations that might correspond to the three horns that are uprooted. We are also going to determine when things happen — whether prior to the beginning of the 70th Week of Daniel, or during it.

In the last article, we determined that Dan 7 and Dan 8 are *parallel scriptures*, each discussing the same set of events. Dan 8 begins with the vision of the Ram and the Goat, material which is not found in Dan. 7. These are two kingdoms that engage in a war at the beginning of the end times.

After the *Goat* overcomes the Ram, it becomes *exceedingly great*. But then its large, prominent horn is *broken off*. We aren't told why, but as we discussed in the last article, perhaps the global superpowers or the UN are intimidated by this powerful Goat kingdom and take action to subdue it. It is at this point that Dan 7 and Dan 8 begin to run in tandem and discuss the same events.

We see the four winds of heaven mentioned, and as we learned in previous articles, these winds are angels. In Dan 7, we also learned that the four winds of heaven stir up the Great Sea, which we determined to be the eastern Mediterranean Sea. We concluded that this *stirring up* was the war between the Ram and the Goat, which results in the subsequent break-up of the Goat empire.

The four winds of heaven then cause the rising of four kingdoms. These kingdoms are referred to as *four Beasts* in Dan 7 and *four horns* in Dan 8. And we learned that there are *six reasons* why these are actually the *same* four kingdoms.

## The Location of the Four Beasts

Since the Little Horn is going to come out of one of these four kingdoms, establishing the locations of the kingdoms becomes crucial.

Let's start at the beginning with the Ram. We are told that this precursor nation occupies the land mass of the Medes and the Persians. This would be modern-day *Iran*. The Goat attacks and defeats the Ram. The Goat (*Yavan*) occupies an area comprising the current territories of eastern Greece and western Turkey, with Istanbul as its principal city. No such nation currently exists, but the Bible tells us one eventually will. So we must speculate as to what it might look like. We expect that it will include all or most of modern Turkey, Greece, and maybe a Balkan country or two.

Istanbul, the major city of this region, was formerly known as Constantinople. This is a very interesting city geopolitically, since it was once the capital of the Islamic Caliphate, the Ottoman Empire. Many Sunni clerics believe to this day that Istanbul is the only legitimate capital for a Sunni Caliphate. In fact, when the Islamic State, or ISIS, established their Caliphate in Raqqa, Syria, the Caliphate was rejected by Sunni clerics because its capital was not in Istanbul.

Turkey's current leader, Erdogan, is a Hitleresque leader who would like nothing better than to be the Caliph of a Caliphate. The desire is certainly there for him to revive the Ottoman Empire. So, as we continue to speculate on what the prophecy in Dan 8 might tell us, Erdogan makes an intriguing candidate to become the prominent horn of the Goat. Perhaps this man — or someone very much like him — will become the first king of a newly-established Caliphate in Yavan.

What might cause the Goat to attack the Ram (Iran), which is the next thing to occur in the prophecy? One possible reason we have already suggested is *religion*. If Shia Iran unveils a man they claim as the 12th Imam — also known as the Mahdi, the savior of the Islamic world — imagine the religious outcry among Sunni Muslims, who have long-expected the Mahdi to come from their branch of Islam!

So, we find that the Goat is *enraged* at the Ram, which we assume are the Shia Iranian-controlled regions. The Shia/Sunni religious divide over who will represent true Islam has simmered for some 1,400 years. Can you imagine how World War III might erupt over this very issue?

Let's see if the Bible supports this scenario:

> *A Ram standing on the bank of the canal. It had two horns, and both horns were high, but one was higher than the other, and the higher one came up last.* **(Dan 8:3-4)**

And look at the following quote attributed to the Mahdi:

> *The truth is with us and in us, and anyone who says this other than us is a liar and a forger.* **Imam Mahdi (AJ)**

## The Rise of the Little Horn

This is one of the most intriguing aspects of the Dan 8 prophecy. Traditionalists who have long-assumed that the Ram corresponds to ancient Persia believe from the Daniel passage that Persia is finally *coming up*, albeit later than the Medes. Mark Davidson, who originally wrote on this topic, had this to say:

> *From a futurist perspective, I suggested they [the horns] were the Supreme Leader of Iran (the Ayatollah) and the Iranian Revolutionary Guard Corps (IRGC). And that the IRGC was the horn that came up later.* **(Mark Davidson)**

Like Davidson, we assume a futurist orientation of the final fulfillment of Dan 8, so the first horn is probably the Supreme Leader (Ayatollah), as he presented. But instead of the Iranian Guard, might the second horn be the *12th Imam,* the one that came up last, was greater, and was given authority? The *12th Imam* certainly would qualify as both a greater horn and one that came up later.

Dan 8 also tells us that the Ram became *great* at this point. Does Iran establish an Imamate (the Shia version of a Caliphate) at this time? This would certainly qualify as becoming *great*. And it would explain why the Goat becomes so enraged. The Goat ultimately does prevail, as it breaks off both horns and tramples the Ram underfoot.

For those of you who have thought that the Ram and the second Beast like-a-Bear are the same creature, a very good reason why they are not was provided by one of our YouTube channel followers: In Dan 7:12 we learned that the Beast like-a-Bear lives on *after* the fourth, terrifying Beast is destroyed and thrown into the lake of fire. This is *after* the return of Christ. But here we see the demise of the Ram, trampled by the Goat. So the Beast like-a-Bear lives on, while the Ram dies. Therefore, the Beast like-a-Bear *cannot* be the Ram.

## The Geography of the Four Beasts

Let's look now at a territorial map of the Middle East and see how it might look after the Goat has defeated the Ram:

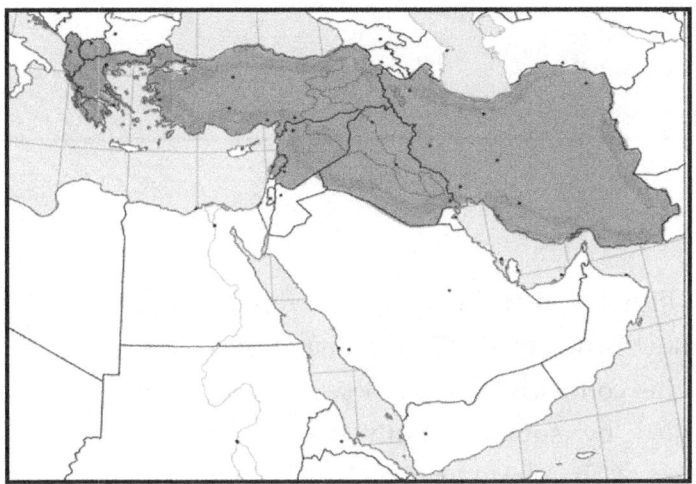

Figure 6-1

It's easy to see why a nation with such extensive geographic reach and political power might cause concern among other countries of the world. Especially if such a nation was controlled by the likes of Erdogan, or someone of a similar mindset.

Now compare our first map with a map of the territories conquered by Alexander the Great:

## The Rise of the Little Horn

**Figure 6-2**

You will notice that the land mass representing the Empire of Alexander is nearly identical to that of the coming Goat empire. From this comparison, we can see that an empire of this size, controlled by someone with the power, ruthlessness, and ambition of an Alexander the Great, would certainly be reason for the nations of the world to worry.

This is precisely what the Bible anticipates happening in Dan 8: The male Goat magnifies himself exceedingly. But as soon as he becomes mighty, the large horn is broken, and the empire is split into four horns, pieces, or kingdoms, which then advance their interests to the four points of the compass — to the north, south, east, and west. It is from one of these horns that the Little Horn will arise.

The four horns are also the four Beasts: One Beast, *like-a-Bear*, in the east, in the lands that once belonged to Persia; one Beast, *like-a-Lion*, to the south, to the lands of Babylon; one Beast, *like-a-Leopard*, occupying land from the former Greek Empire in the north; and one *terrifying Beast* in the west. now holding land that was once the property of Assyria, the people of Nimrod.

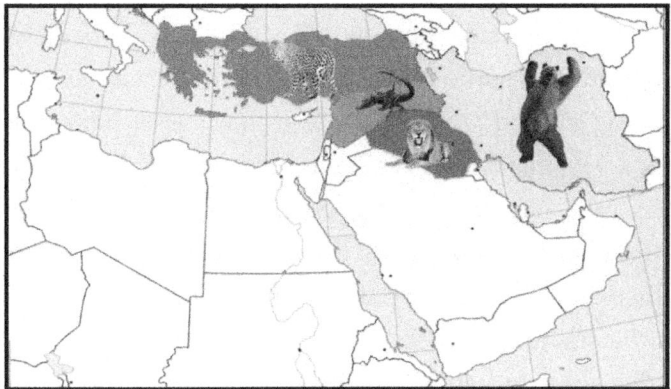

Figure 6-3

Four new kingdoms, from one broken horn, all leading to one Little Horn: The beginning of the Antichrist's career.

## Possible Identity of the 10 Horns

Scripture tells us that the Little Horn arises *out of* one of the four horns of the Goat. But before the Little Horn arises, we are told in Dan 7 that there are actually *10 horns to the Beast Empire*.

At the moment the winds of heaven stir up the Gentile nations, which leads to the break-up of the Goat into four, smaller horns, are the six other horns established as well? Is the 10-horned Beast Empire developed at this same time by the same powers that split up the Goat Nation? Perhaps. That is our guess, and it makes perfect sense: Although the global powers might step in to remove an offending national figure (the prominent horn) and to re-align national borders, they would be unlikely to completely eliminate nations. Besides, we find that *all 10 horns are* in place at the time the Little Horn arises.

So, what are the identities of the other six horns? Although naming-names remains somewhat subjective, I believe that scripture identifies some of them for us. The Beast has *10 horns*; but, as we learned earlier, it also has *seven heads*, which represent *seven kingdoms*. We have *previously identified* these as Egypt, Assyria, Babylon, Persia, Greece, Rome, and the Islamic Caliphate. Four of these heads are already included within the area which will be occupied by the four Beasts: Assyria, Babylon, Persia, and Greece. And we should assume that the 10 horns will also include the remaining three heads, since the final Beast Empire has seven heads and 10 horns.

Therefore, we should add horns for Egypt and the Islamic Caliphate, which began in what is now Saudi Arabia. That leaves *Rome* as the only head unaccounted for. Do we add a horn for Rome in Italy? Maybe and maybe not. As we explained earlier, the eastern half of the Roman Empire, the Byzantine Empire, was based in Turkey, so that head is already accounted for.

Let's continue to try and figure out all the horns. The Kingdom of *Jordan* is mentioned in several end times texts (e.g. Dan 11:41) and it's surrounded by all of these other horns that have been identified. We think that Jordan is a *likely seventh horn*.

In an end times passage that we've already looked at, Ezek 38-39, a number of other nations are listed, including Magog, Gomer, and Beth-Togarmah, all of which are thought to be part of present-day Turkey, and all of which are accounted for by horns already. Persia is accounted for as well. The ancient nation of Cush is thought to be *Libya*, and Put is thought to be *Sudan*. These might be candidates for the *eighth and ninth horns*.

We have one horn to go. The lands of Meshach and Tubal are typically thought to be in an area *just north of Turkey*, around the Caspian and Black Seas. Might this be the *10th horn*? We admit that we are the least confident about this identity. But it seems a sensible choice.

This arrangement of nations produces a 10-horned confederacy completely surrounding Israel for hundreds of miles in every direction. Let's envision what this might look like in the following map:

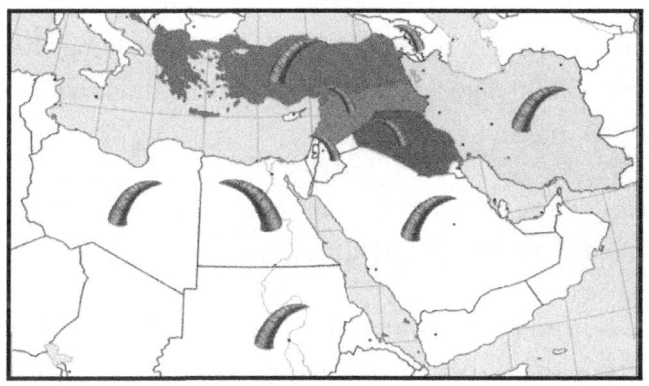

Figure 6-4

After the 10 horns are established, the Little Horn is now about to begin his career of conquest. He *plucks out three* of the 10 horns by the roots:

> *While I was contemplating the horns, behold, another horn, a little one, came up among them, and three of the first horns were pulled out by the roots before it.* **(Dan 7:8)**

## The Rise of the Little Horn

Before we examine which three horns these might be, let's stop for a moment and consider what it means to *pluck them out by the roots*. In order for the Little Horn to pluck out three of the original horns, it must mean that these horns are independent of each other. It may also mean that they are aligned in some form of confederacy or alliance. Therefore, the Little Horn cannot yet be in charge of them. Otherwise, there would be no need to pluck them out.

When we hear the term *plucked out by the roots*, we usually think of an uprooted tree. But this is different. The horns are not uprooted and eliminated, although we have heard many excellent Bible scholars say regarding this point that *there are now three fewer horns*. In Revelation we read that all 10 of the horns *hand over power* to the Beast, thereby implying that there are indeed *still 10 horns* at that time. So this must be a *different* type of plucking up by the roots.

> *He will come in a time of tranquility and seize the kingdom by intrigue.* **(Dan 11:21)**

This time of tranquility comes after the division into 10 horns. It is at this time that Little Horn seizes the kingdom by intrigue or deception. Since we now understand that there are still 10 horns when he's done, does he *uproot the existing* three kings and place his own *puppet rulers in their place*? To me this seems to be what the scriptures imply. How else do we *maintain* a total of 10 rulers?

So what three horns does Little Horn replace? We are given *two clues* about how this intrigue occurs. *First*, in Dan 8 we are given the *directions* in which Little Horn becomes great: *To the south, to the east, and toward the beautiful land. Second,* we remember that the Beast is a composite of a Leopard, a Bear, and a Lion. So we think it's safe to assume that these other three horns are involved. Rev 13 also tells us that the Beast is "like-a-Leopard," that its body is that of a Leopard, and to us that means the Leopard predominates.

Let's now fit the clues together. If the Beast like-a-Leopard predominates, then perhaps the Little Horn comes out of that horn. We then find, as recorded in Dan 8, that he first goes to the *south*, then to the *east*, and then back *towards the beautiful land*, which is Israel.

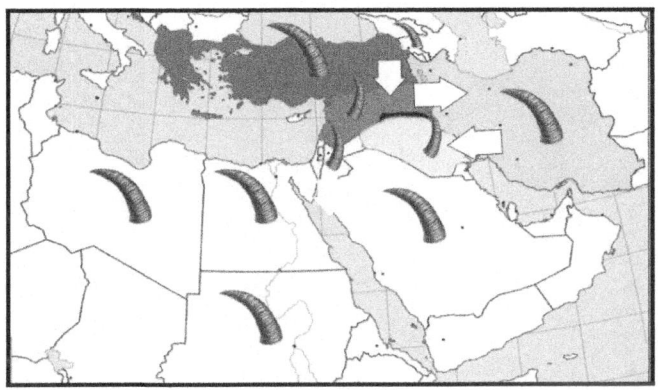

Figure 6-5

Moving south, the Beast like-a-Leopard would be into the land of *Nimrod*, where the *demon Beast* is based. We are then told that he goes east into the land of the Beast like-a-Bear. Finally, from there he goes due west, back towards Israel, the beautiful land, into the territory of the Beast like-a-Lion.

We believe that scripture perfectly aligns the movement of Little Horn with future nations destined to take part in this end times territorial imperative. We have constructed exactly what the Bible describes. The Beast like-a-Leopard predominates (Rev 13:2). The Leopard has four heads (Dan 7:6), or acquired influence, over the other three horns, and it is given dominion

## The Rise of the Little Horn

(Dan 7:6). We know the direction and order of conquest. But when does Little Horn do this in relation to the 70th Week of Daniel - before or after it begins? We'll review the career of Little Horn in detail in the next article.

## Article Seven

### The Little Horn's Brutal Career

The visions in Dan 7 and 8 detail the short, brutal career of the Antichrist, otherwise known as the Little Horn. After Daniel received these visions, he was shaken and sick for days. In that same spirit, we should consider these visions with all seriousness, yet with the confidence that comes from knowing from scripture that Jesus will triumph in the end.

In the last article, we determined what nations might make up the 10 horns. And as we have already learned, a critical, but often overlooked, point is that the Antichrist arises only after the 10 horns are *fully established*, and not before:

> *When I was contemplating the horns behold another horn a little one came up among them.* **(Dan 7:8)**

From this passage we can and should assume two facts about the Little Horn. *First*, he is a little or *insignificant* horn. He isn't a well-known leader. *Second*, he doesn't arise until *after* the 10 horns are in place. This should eliminate all well-known leaders in the world at this time. It is most likely the Antichrist is someone from the Middle East who is completely unknown right now. So instead of getting caught up in the name-guessing game of trying to identify the Antichrist, we should instead remain watchful for the signs of this coming Man of Sin.

After the Little Horn arises, he *plucks three* other horns out by the roots. We discussed this in the previous article. We then learn something absolutely incredible that allows us to *timestamp* the

## The Little Horn's Brutal Career

events associated with the rise of Little Horn. Daniel's vision takes him into the Throne Room of God:

> *I kept looking until thrones were set up, and the Ancient of Days took His seat; His vesture was like white snow and the hair of His head like pure wool. His throne was ablaze with flames, its wheels were a burning fire. A river of fire was flowing and coming out from before Him; thousands upon thousands were attending Him, and myriads upon myriads were standing before Him.* **(Dan. 7:9-10)**

How does this scene of God in His Glory allow us to timestamp the rise of the Little Horn? This may not seem like a familiar scene to most, but this passage in Daniel about God's Throne Room reflects the *exact same events* found in — and expanded upon — in Rev 4 and 5. In Daniel, there are *two verses*. In Revelation, *two chapters*. In Daniel, the prophet saw the vision. In Revelation it was John. Beyond that, there are an amazing *five, exact similarities* between these sections of scripture, which we will summarize in a moment.

What makes this a key *timestamp* is that the vision in Revelation occurs *prior* to the opening of a 7-sealed scroll, which is acknowledged by most to be the beginning of the 70th Week of Daniel. If this vision is the *same* as the one in Daniel, then *everything* that happens in Dan 7 and 8 *prior* to this vision also occurs prior to the 70th Week. This is a *key insight* and one of the most significant time markers in the career of the Little Horn.

Let me state that again. If the vision of the Throne Room is prior to the beginning of a 70th Week, then everything in Dan 7 and 8 before that are also *before* the 70th Week. This means that the following events which we learned about in the last article *all* take place *before* the 70th Week: The war between the Ram and the Goat (Iran and Turkey), the formation of the four Beasts/four horns from the breakup of the Goat, the Little Horn arising, and the plucking out of three of the horns to re-form the four into a single kingdom. Wow!

Now, let's look at the scriptures and confirm the *five similarities* that show Dan 7:9-10 are the same as Rev 4-5 (note that one of the references is to Rev 6-8):

| Event | Dan | Rev |
|---|---|---|
| Thrones placed | Dan 7:9 | Rev 4:4 |
| Lord on His Throne | Dan 7:9 | Rev 4:2 |
| Flames from His Throne | Dan 7:9-10 | Rev 4:5 |
| Thousands of attendants | Dan 7:10 | Rev 5:11 |
| Books were opened | Dan 7:10 | Rev 6-8 |

Figure 7-1

Daniel's vision and John's vision were the same; it's just that John was given more detail, or managed to record more of what he saw. In the *first three similarities*, we see that the prophets record the Thrones being placed, then we see the Lord upon His Throne, then flames or lightning flashed from beneath the Throne.

The *fourth similarity* records the *number* of the Lord's angel attendants. The Greek phrases used in the Greek Septuagint version of Daniel and in Revelation for this number are *identical*: *myriads myriadōn kai chiliades chiliadōn*, which means *myriads of myriads and thousands of thousands*. Direct quotes are one way that the Bible indicates that two things are the *same*.

Finally, in the *fifth similarity*, the books were opened in Dan 7, and the 7-sealed scroll is opened in Rev 6-8. These five similarities *imply* that Daniel and John saw the *same* vision.

## The Books Were Opened

Now, when we read that the books were opened, the *7-sealed scroll* was *only one* of these books (scrolls). What exactly are these scrolls, and why are they opened at this point?

We know that the books are opened for *judgment*, as we learn from Revelation:

> *Then I saw thrones, and they sat on them, and judgment was given to them.* **(Rev 20: 4)**

These are the same Thrones as recorded in Dan 7 and Rev 4.

But what exactly are these *books*? As I've indicated, the 7-sealed scroll is *only one* of the books opened. This same phrase, *the books were opened*, appears in Revelation, and it is explained there:

> *And I saw the dead, the great and the small, standing before the throne, and **books were opened**; and another book was opened, which is the book of life; and the dead were judged from the things which were written in the books, according to their deeds.* **(Rev 20:12)**

These *same books* are opened at the Second Resurrection. We can assume, then, that these books are also opened at the First Resurrection, which occurs at the coming, or *parousia*, of Jesus (1 Cor 15:23). This event occurs in the second half of the 70th Week of Daniel. Prior to each Resurrection, a *Book of Deeds* is opened, as well as the *Book of life*. The dead written in the Book of Life are resurrected to life. The unrepentant dead are not, but instead await the Second Resurrection:

> *Everyone who is found written in the book, will be rescued. Many of those who sleep in the dust of the ground will awake, these to everlasting life, but the others to disgrace and everlasting contempt.* **(Dan 12:1-2)**

So the books that will be opened in Dan 7:10 are a *Book of Deeds*, the *Book of Life* and the *7-sealed scroll*. Three books in all.

Although Daniel and John were observing the same events in similar visions, they lived 600 years apart. Yet there is an *exact* match in the details from the visions of both Dan 7:9-10 and Rev 4-8.

From which we conclude that all of the events in Dan 7 — and the related events in Dan 8 prior to Dan 7:9-10 — occur *prior to* the 70th Week of Daniel. This includes the commotion in the Gentile nations, the Goat overcoming the Ram, the splitting of the Goat kingdom into four Beasts or horns, and the first three Beasts being overcome by the intrigue of the Little Horn.

Jesus alluded to these events in an end times parable in the Gospel of Luke, the parable of the fig tree and all the trees:

> *Behold the fig tree (Israel) and all the trees (the gentile nations round about) as soon as they put forth leaves, you see it and know for yourselves that summer is now near. So you also, when you see these things happening, recognize that the kingdom of God is near.* **(Luke 21:29-31)**

Scripture interprets scripture. All of the trees (nations) need to be in place in order for the 70th Week to begin. Israel is already sprouting leaves; but the Gentile nations need to experience *commotion* before the 70th Week can begin.

Many Christians are aware that parallel parables exist in the Gospels of Matthew and Mark. In this case, the two parables only discuss the *Fig Tree*. Consequently, many Christians have been led to believe that the reformation of Israel in 1948 was all that was needed for the 70th Week to begin: The Fig Tree is sprouting leaves. This is an inaccurate understanding. Luke's version of the parable demonstrates that the Gentile nations, the four Beasts, must also be in place prior to the 70th Week. *This is an important insight.*

## The Brutal Career of the Little Horn

The vast majority of remaining information which we learn about the Little Horn comes from Dan 8. There we see that he will destroy to an *extraordinary* degree:

> *His power will be mighty, but not by his own power. And he will destroy to an extraordinary degree and prosper and perform his will. He will destroy mighty men and the holy people and through his shrewdness he will cause deceit to succeed by his influence. And he will magnify himself in his heart, and he will destroy many while they are at ease.* **(Dan 8:24-25)**

In Dan 11 we encounter a similar passage:

> *He will take action against the strongest of fortresses with the help of a foreign god; he will give great honor to those who acknowledge him and will cause them to rule*

*over the many, and will parcel out land for a price.*
**(Dan 11:39)**

The Little Horn will destroy to an extraordinary degree. How does he accomplish this? The *demon* that possesses him supernaturally assists him. People in Western nations believe they may be safe and secure behind their military might, but both of these passages indicate that the Antichrist will be powerful enough to overcome the strongest of foes because of assistance from a demonic power *(foreign god)* — and not because of his own ability. Israel and the USA may think they are safe, but according to scripture, they are not. Supernatural power trumps earthly power.

*Destroy to an extraordinary degree* is a frightening concept. Might it imply the use of nuclear weapons? It might. Might Little Horn use these in a surprise attack? Possibly. Scripture says he will destroy many while they are *at ease*. This certainly implies that those affected will be unaware and ill-prepared.

The passage in Dan 11 also demonstrates that the Antichrist will hand out favors to those loyal to him, which, according to scripture, may include placing them in positions of authority over others and offering them land acquired thru victory, at a price. It appears, then, that in addition to the help provided by demons, Little Horn will have help from *earthly forces*, as well. How might this be?

We can only speculate. Islamic writings indicate that a man will arise in the end times named *Isa*. Muslims believe Isa will say that he is the *historic Jesus*, returned to earth. They also expect Isa to announce that Judgment Day has come; and he will call all Muslims, both radical and moderate, to rise up in *world-wide jihad*. Eerily, Jesus spoke of something similar:

## The Little Horn's Brutal Career

> *Many will come in My name, saying, 'I am He,' and, 'The time is near.' Do not go after them. When you hear of wars and disturbances, do not be terrified.* **(Luke 21:8-9)**

Jesus tells us a *false prophet* will come claiming to be Him, the historic Jesus, and that this false prophet will proclaim *the time is near*. What time is that? Could it be the Judgment Day Muslims expect Isa to proclaim? Perhaps.

If a man named Isa *claims* to be the real Jesus, we can be absolutely certain that he won't be. He will be a Muslim. Per Muslim doctrine, he will deny that Jesus ever was divine and will dispute His death on the cross. He will claim that Jesus was merely a prophet, *not* the Son of God. If Isa arises, he will *very likely be the false prophet.*

We see a prophecy of similar events in a passage from the Bible:

> *Then I saw another beast coming up out of the earth; and he had two horns like a lamb and he spoke as a dragon.* **(Rev 13:11)**

The Beast comes out of the *sea*, which we have seen represents the Gentile nations. Meanwhile, this false prophet comes from the *land*, which is likely Israel. The false prophet has *two horns*, which might be the houses of *Judah and Israel*. We are also told that he *looks like a lamb*, which could be the *Lamb of God*. But he *speaks like Satan*. This seems a perfect fit with Isa; *if* he does exist at some point, this sounds like a perfect description of what we expect from him.

Immediately after the rise of this evil character, Jesus warns us about wars and disturbances, which include rebellions and fighting in the streets. Are a portion of these disturbances the jihad this false prophet may be inciting? Jesus says that we are not to be frightened by any of it. I suspect that the reason Jesus warns us is because, by any measure, 1.5 billion Muslims worldwide rising in jihad would be an *absolutely terrifying* phenomenon. Are these among those that Little Horn rewards? Perhaps they are.

Dan 11 also speaks of some of the particulars of the Little Horn's military campaign:

> *At the end time the king of the South will collide with him, and the king of the North will storm against him (the King of the South) with chariots, with horsemen and with many ships; and he will enter countries, overflow them and pass through.* **(Dan 11:40)**

By this point in the narrative, the Little Horn will have utilized intrigue to acquire influence over the entire area that was once the Goat kingdom. The size of this kingdom is similar to the ancient *Seleucid Empire* that formed during the wars of the Diadochi after the death of Alexander the Great. In the Bible, the rulers of this region were known as the *Kings of the North*.

These kings were in opposition to the other major kingdom that formed out of Alexander's realm, the *Ptolemaic Kingdom*, the *Kings of the South*. Dan 11:40 seems to indicate that these ancient wars will repeat in the end times, and that the Antichrist will ultimately triumph.

Let's return to our map of the ten horns to visualize this aspect of the career of the Little Horn:

## The Little Horn's Brutal Career

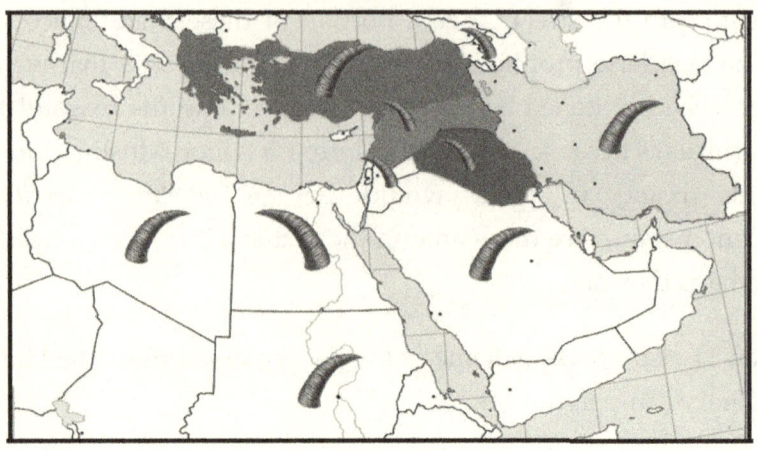

Figure 7-2

Who might the *King of the South* be? Looking at the map, there are five northern horns, primarily in the dark-shaded region, that probably represent the territory controlled by the *King of the North*. There are also five southern horns. Might the southern horns act as one group to oppose the aggression of the Little Horn and the northern alliance of horns? Maybe the southern horns will form their own alliance and their leader will become the King of the South.

Chapter 11 of the book of Daniel mentions some of these southern horns:

> *He will also enter the Beautiful Land, and many countries will fall; but these will be rescued out of his hand: Edom, Moab and the foremost of the sons of Ammon. Then he will stretch out his hand against other countries, and the land of Egypt will not escape. But he will gain control over the hidden treasures of gold and silver and over all the precious things of Egypt; and Libyans (Cush) and Ethiopians (Put) will follow at his heels.* **(Dan 11:41-43)**

From this highly descriptive text, we can see that Egypt, Libya (Cush), and Sudan (Put) will fall to the Antichrist. But three people-groups *don't fall* into his clutches: Edom, Moab and Ammon, which most believe are, collectively, the Kingdom of Jordan. Therefore, this area will initially remain beyond the control of the Antichrist.

Now, Saudi Arabia is not mentioned directly; however, we know that at some point *all ten* horns *give their power* to the Antichrist. So, these horns only *temporarily* remain outside his control:

> *The ten horns which you saw are ten kings who have not yet received a kingdom, but they receive authority as kings with the beast for one hour. These have one purpose, and they give their power and authority to the beast.* **(Rev 17:12-13)**

We know, therefore, that eventually *all five* southern horns succumb to the Antichrist. This alignment with him most likely takes place at the midpoint of the 70th Week of Daniel, at the Abomination of Desolation.

Let's see what else happens at the midpoint. First, Dan 8 tells us that the stars of heaven fall to the earth:

> *It grew up to the host of heaven and caused some of the host and some of the stars to fall to the earth, and it trampled them down.* **(Dan 8:10)**

Is this the same event as we see in Rev 12?

> *And the great dragon was thrown down, the serpent of old who is called the devil and Satan, who deceives the*

> *whole world; he was thrown down to the earth, and his angels were thrown down with him.* **(Rev 12:9)**

It appears the events in Dan 8 and Rev 12 are *both* describing Satan and his fallen angels being thrown out of heaven. It is at this same time that Little Horn is likely to take over the Temple:

> *It even magnified itself to be equal with the Commander of the host; and it removed the regular sacrifice from Him, and the place of His sanctuary was thrown down. And on account of transgression the host will be given over to the horn along with the regular sacrifice.* **(Dan 8:11-12)**

As we can see, Little Horn exalts himself over Jesus, the Commander of the Host, and ends regular sacrifice in the Temple. This is, of course, the same event in Daniel that many are already familiar with:

> *For half of the week he shall put an end to sacrifice and offering. And on the wing of abominations shall come one who makes desolate, until the decreed end is poured out on the desolator.* **(Dan 9:27)**

This same Abomination of Desolation is also mentioned in Dan 11:

> *Forces from him shall appear and profane the temple and fortress, and shall take away the regular burnt offering. And they shall set up the abomination that makes desolate.* **(Dan 11:31)**

And Jesus mentions this central event, as well:

> *So when you see the abomination of desolation spoken of by the prophet Daniel, standing in the holy place...* **(Matt 24:15)**

Jesus's mention of the Abomination is *key*, because it requires that the Abomination takes place *after* Jesus's lifetime.

Paul also mentions this central event:

> *The man of lawlessness is revealed, the son of destruction, who opposes and exalts himself against every so-called god or object of worship, so that he takes his seat in the temple of God, proclaiming himself to be God.* **(2 Thess 2:3-4)**

Paul is clear that this event is the revealing of the Man of Sin, the Antichrist. Although the book of Daniel includes a number of signs associated with the Little Horn that may point to this man or that man as the Antichrist, we have maintained consistently that we cannot be certain until he sits in the Temple of God. There will be many wanna-be, false messiahs. Some exist as we write this book. But the man who sits in the Temple will be the Antichrist. This is a *key understanding*.

## The Little Horn's Purpose

The Little Horn is intent on receiving the *worship due Go*d, taking it for himself and Satan. Rev 13 tells us that there are four means by which the Beast seeks to receive worship. This is a *crucial point*. The Beast doesn't receive worship because he is deemed worthy to be the Messiah of Israel, as many claim. He isn't worshipped because the Jews accept him. No, he receives worship out of deception and fear.

In fact, Jesus said:

> *I have come in My Father's name, and you do not receive Me; if another comes in his own name, you will receive him.* **(John 5:43)**

Jesus came in His Father's name, Yehovah. The Little Horn will come in his own name. *Coming in the Father's name* has two meanings. *First*, it means that Jesus came as the Son of the Jewish God. By coming in his own name, the Antichrist will not come representing the Jewish God. *Second*, the phrase also means that Jesus *fulfilled* the biblical requirements to be the Messiah. By not coming in the Father's name, the Antichrist will not fulfill the specific biblical requirements to be the Messiah. For both reasons, the Antichrist is precluded from representing the Jewish God. These points are very poorly understood.

Let's now look at the four means by which the Little Horn, as the Antichrist, will extract worship. *First*, he will do so by deception, using signs and wonders performed by the false prophet:

> *And he makes the earth and those who dwell in it to worship the first beast, whose fatal wound was healed. He performs great signs, so that he even makes fire come down out of heaven to the earth in the presence of men.* **(Rev 13:12-13)**

Jesus referred to these signs, as well, and told us they will be incredibly convincing:

> *For false Christs and false prophets will arise and will show great signs and wonders, so as to mislead, if possible, even the elect.* **(Matt 24:24)**

Those who see these signs *with their eyes and not by faith* will be completely convinced of these signs. Paul also refers to these signs, indicating that they are empowered by Satan:

> *The one whose coming is in accord with the activity of Satan, with all power and signs and false wonders, and with all the deception of wickedness for those who perish, because they did not receive the love of the truth so as to be saved.* **(2 Thess 2:9-10)**

The *second* means by which the Little Horn receives worship is through his ability to wage war:

> *They worshiped the beast, saying, "Who is like the beast, and who is able to wage war with him?"* **(Rev 13:4)**

Why is the ability of the Antichrist to wage war any different than that of other evil world rulers? Why does it inspire worship? Remember Dan 8 and Dan 11 tell us that the Antichrist is *empowered* by the demonic Beast to wage war. The world will likely recognize the *supernatural nature* of his victories, and they'll worship him because of the other-worldly source of his military exploits. He will likely win when it appears humanly impossible.

The *third* means by which Little Horn gains worship is via economic manipulation. The false prophet implements the mark of the Beast:

> *He provides that no one will be able to buy or to sell, except the one who has the mark.* **(Rev 13:17)**

No one will be able to participate in the world system of commerce without taking the mark of the Beast. Those who

## The Little Horn's Brutal Career

have not prepared for this action and those who are unwilling to go *off the grid* will worship the Beast in order to survive.

The *fourth* and final means by which the Antichrist receives worship will be by *threatening* the inhabitants of the world with death unless they worship him:

> *And it was given to him (the false prophet) to give breath to the image of the beast, so that the image of the beast would even speak and cause as many as do not worship the image of the beast to be killed.* **(Rev 13:15)**

So an evil *image* of the Beast will be constructed by the earth dwellers, and the false prophet will give it breath and the ability to speak. Those who don't worship the image will be killed. The *fear of physical death* will inspire many who were not moved to worship by the first three means to finally pay homage to the image of the Beast. This worship will, as we know from Rev 14, be the *spiritual death* of those who may have once professed to be Christians:

> *... If anyone worships the beast and his image, and receives a mark on his forehead or on his hand, he also will drink of the wine of the wrath of God ... And the smoke of their torment goes up forever and ever; they have no rest day and night, those who worship the beast and his image, and whoever receives the mark of his name.* **(Rev 14:9-11)**

So, we see that the career of the Little Horn will center on the receiving of worship by these *four means*: Deception by false signs and wonders, supernatural military victories, economic control over all buying and selling, and fear of death. None of these means of acquiring worship indicate a *worthiness* to be worshipped or to be Messiah. Rather, they are deceptive and brutal in their nature.

## The End of the Little Horn's Career

But, finally, the rule of Little Horn will come to an end. As we learned in Dan 7:9-10, the heavenly court will sit in judgment. The books will be opened. The Antichrist will be defeated. As we read in Dan 8:

> *He shall be broken — but by no human hand.* **(Dan 8:25)**

Jesus will destroy the kingdom, kill the Little Horn, and throw the demon into the Lake of Fire.

The death of the Little Horn brings up a very interesting point. It has been said that the Gog of Ezek 38-39 may be the Antichrist. Not everyone agrees, however, because in Ezek 39 we see that Gog is killed and buried, while we know from Rev 19 that the Beast is thrown alive into the Lake of Fire. To many, this is an irreconcilable difference. But, now that we know that the *Beast is a man, a demon, and a kingdom,* all at the same time, we see that this scenario is possible. There is no irreconcilable difference. The Beast can be both killed and thrown alive into the Lake of Fire. If God wills it, both can be true at the same time. The man is killed and buried and the demon is thrown alive in the Lake of Fire.

## Article Eight

### Will the Tribulation Begin with a Peace Treaty?

One of the most widely held end times views is that the final 7-year Tribulation period, or 70th Week of Daniel, will begin with a Middle East peace treaty. No matter what a person's other end times views may be, most hold this position. And given recent news media attention related to the Middle East peace process, it's easy to see why this issue remains in the forefront of people's minds. In this article, we're going to explore the biblical basis for this widely-held belief.

Before we dissect this issue, let's first think through its implications. *First*, many believe the rapture will occur *prior* to the Tribulation. So, *if* the 70th Week truly does begin with a peace treaty, the rapture would have to take place *prior to* this treaty. This relationship between a peace treaty and a Pretrib. rapture causes those who support this theory to anticipate the rapture any time a peace plan is discussed. Social media then is filled with such claims — which, of course, reflects poorly on Christianity when nothing happens.

*Second*, the beginning of the 70th Week is like the two-minute warning in football — the time when everything changes and new strategies are put into place. Get the timing of the 70th Week wrong, and you are either totally unprepared for what will happen, or you will be totally disillusioned when nothing at all does happen.

*Third*, because most also believe that the *Antichrist* will be the one to broker this peace plan, the assumption is that one of the main characters in the negotiations must be the Antichrist.

## Will the Tribulation Begin With a Peace Treaty?

Trump, Kushner, and Netanyahu have all been implicated at one time or another. But if the world is mistaken about this issue, the *real* Antichrist may lurk undetected in the background, while attention is focused on the wrong individuals.

### What the Bible Says About a Peace Treaty

As a way of supporting that the 7-year 70th Week will begin with a peace plan, it would be nice if its proponents could quote from scripture, perhaps directly from Jesus. Unfortunately, Jesus said nothing about a peace treaty. When Jesus was specifically asked by his disciples about what signs would precede His coming, there was *nothing* in there about a peace plan. For something that has gained such popularity, don't you find that more than a little bit odd?

A peace treaty would be a widely recognized and highly celebrated event, an obvious sign. But when specifically asked about signs, Jesus said *nothing* about it. If this was indeed an important sign — in fact *the* crucial one marking the beginning of the 70th Week — why did Jesus fail to mention it?

Let me state that again because it's a significant point, albeit mostly ignored. Why did Jesus *not mention* a peace treaty when specifically asked for the signs of His coming? Did He desire to deceive us? Hardly! A better explanation is, quite simply, that a peace treaty is *not* one of the signs.

The book of Revelation — which essentially provides a chronology of end times events — also says nothing about a peace plan. So, we find that the most extensive and descriptive teaching on end times events says nothing about a treaty. Again, don't you find that strange?

And there's more! Paul's Epistles also contain nothing about a peace plan or treaty. Now in fairness, Paul does mention *peace and safety* in 1 Thess. However, this statement is made in relationship to the Day of the Lord, when the sun and moon are darkened, and when sudden destruction in the form of fire and brimstone occur. It is *not* made in relation to the beginning of the Tribulation, which we know is simply the beginning of the time of false prophets and false messiahs — and not about destruction.

In fact, the entire New Testament is silent on the issue of a peace plan before the Tribulation. So, if Jesus didn't mention it, John didn't mention it, and Paul didn't mention it, why do the vast majority of Christians *expect a peace plan* to usher in the Tribulation, the 70th Week of Daniel?

The answer may surprise you. Apparently, numerous Old Testament passages *seem* to indicate a false peace is established in the end times. In Ezek 38, Gog attacks Israel when the nation is living in *un-walled* villages, implying the Jews were living in peace. Psm 35:20 and 28:3 both mention deceitful foreigners who *promise peace*.

Additionally, Isaiah contains this very famous passage about a false reliance on a foreign power, rather than trusting God:

> *Because you have said, "We have made a covenant with death, and with Sheol we have made a pact. The overwhelming scourge will not reach us when it passes by, for we have made falsehood our refuge and we have concealed ourselves with deception."* **(Isa 28:15)**

Some or all of these passages may refer to the end times. We actually do believe that a false peace will exist at that time. But there is a *problem*. None of the scripture passages specifically indicate that the false peace occurs at the *inception* of the 70th Week. It could be negotiated before the 70th Week begins or after. Taking the position that a peace plan is something which the world should expect as the *beginning* of the final 7-year period in the history of mankind is *not supported* anywhere in the Bible.

In fact, there is only *one passage* in scripture that even remotely indicates that the 70th Week begins with a peace treaty:

> *And he will make a firm covenant with the many for one week.* **(Dan 9:27)**

That's it. In the entire Bible, *only this one* passage implies a peace treaty begins the *70th Week* of Daniel. That last phrase is key — the 70th Week of Daniel. The prophet Daniel was given the most specific timeline for the last seven years in the Bible. And it is in Daniel that we find this single mention of a possible peace plan.

## Daniel's Anonymous *He*

If we carefully examine this partial verse, we find that an anonymous *he* makes, confirms, or strengthens a covenant with an equally anonymous *many* for the entire seven years of Daniel's final 7-year period. The most common understanding of this passage is that the *he* is the Antichrist, and the *many* are the Jews.

That isn't the only understanding, however; and many have spent their lives searching for a confirming scripture. The reason they have looked for a second scripture is that, as Paul tells us, a fact is only confirmed upon the testimony of two or three witnesses:

> *Every fact is to be confirmed by the testimony of two or three witnesses.* **(2 Cor 13:1)**

So far, the search for the elusive confirming scripture has been in vain; and we are left with this solitary half-verse as evidence.

Now, we would usually accept whatever scripture says as valid, even without confirmation. But if the verse is unclear as to its meaning — as we see in this situation — then only the confirmation of another scripture will ensure that we understand the true meaning. Scripture interprets scripture.

The historically-popular position of a peace plan was established while the book of Daniel was still sealed. So, although most Christians still believe that Dan 9:27 concerns a peace treaty between the Antichrist and Israel, we need to be suspicious. Yet, most are *adamant* that this is an absolute truth.

So if you're in the *adamant camp*, let's take a look at Dan. 9:27 again, because everything hinges on this one verse; there is no second witness. Worse yet, it actually hinges on a single word, the word *he*, which most assume means the Antichrist.

But rather than looking at this single, *partial verse*, let's *expand* our view to include the *entire verse*, thereby increasing our chances of understanding the meaning of the scripture *in context*. When we do so, we find something fascinating:

> *And **he** will make a firm covenant with the many for one week, but in the middle of the week **he** will put a stop to sacrifice and grain offering; and on the wing of abominations will come **one who make desolate**, even*

> until a complete destruction, one that is decreed, is poured out on the **one who makes desolate**. **(Dan 9:27)**

Wow! There are actually *two characters*, not one. First, there is the individual we have previously been analyzing, the anonymous *he*, who does two things: He makes or strengthens a covenant, and he puts a stop to sacrifice and offering. But then we learn that there is a *second* character who is called *one who makes desolate*. These are likely *not* the same person!

We see that the *one who makes desolate* comes on the wings of abomination, and a complete destruction is poured out on him. Now, almost everyone believes that this second character is the Antichrist. But notice the phrase, *on the wings of abomination will come one who makes desolate*. This passage implies, or rather demands, that this character makes his debut *after* the midpoint of the 70th Week. If this character enters the scene after the midpoint, and if he is given a different name than the anonymous, *he*, they *are likely not the same person*, are they?

No, they probably aren't! So who is the anonymous *he*? Daniel tells us there will be a covenant that our mysterious *he* will either make or strengthen for the *entire* 7-year 70th Week. *He* is a pronoun, and all pronouns must refer back to someone *earlier* in the text. It must have an antecedent.

> *Then after the sixty-two weeks the Messiah will be cut off and have nothing, and the people* **of the prince who is to come** *will destroy the city and the sanctuary. . . And he will make a firm covenant with the many for one week.* **(Dan 9:26, 27)**

The last person referred to in the prophecy before the anonymous *he* is the *prince who is to come*, in Dan 9:26. *That* is the antecedent. Our mysterious *he* must be referring back to the last person mentioned — and that is the *prince who is to come*.

This is why nearly everyone says that the *he* is the Antichrist. It was his people who destroyed the city of Jerusalem and the Temple in AD 70. Only an evil prince could have done those things, isn't that right? It seems like an open and shut case to most scholars.

## The People of the Prince Who Is to Come

Maybe not. Let's think through this clearly. The *prince who is to come* is an end times figure. He is the one who makes the covenant during the 70th Week of Daniel. He did *not* personally destroy the city and the Temple in AD 70. Rather, it was the *people* of the prince who is to come who physically destroyed the Temple. The scripture isn't telling us whether the prince is evil or good. It is a neutral statement. Dan 9:26 appears to be identifying the *ethnicity* of the prince. Scholars have assumed the prince who is to come will likely arise from the *same ethnic nationality* as those who destroyed the city and the Temple.

So, who are the people of the prince who is to come? Are they Romans? Most people think so. The Roman Legions certainly did destroy both Jerusalem and the Temple in AD 70. But does that make the *Roman Legion* the people of the prince who is to come?

Bible scholar and my good friend, Joel Richardson, has suggested that although the armies that destroyed Jerusalem carried the standard of Rome, they were *not primarily of Roman ethnicity*. Rather they were *conscripts* from the Middle East under the direction of a Roman general — they were primarily *Arabs*.

Richardson has done extensive research on the ethnic make-up of the various Legions that besieged Jerusalem during this period, and you can find the results of that research in his classic book, *Mideast Beast* (2012). Based on Richardson's findings, it seems quite likely that Syrian troops were the ones who set the Temple on fire.

However, there is a third, almost unthinkable option presented in the scriptures. Who does the Bible say was responsible for Jerusalem's destruction? Jesus was very clear that the *Jews themselves* were responsible for Jerusalem's downfall:

> *When He approached Jerusalem, He saw the city and wept over it, saying, "If you had known in this day, even you, the things which make for peace! But now they have been hidden from your eyes. For the days will come upon you when your enemies will throw up a barricade against you, and surround you and hem you in on every side, and they will level you to the ground and your children within you, and they will not leave in you one stone upon another,* **because you did not recognize the time of your visitation.** **(Luke 19:41-44)**

This statement echoes the prophecy of Hosea:

> **O Israel, thou hast destroyed thyself;** *but in me is thine help.* **(Hos 13:9)**

This biblical position was also supported by Flavious Josephus, the famous first century historian and witness to the destruction of Jerusalem. Josephus recorded that the *Jews* may not have actually thrown the torch that burned the Temple, but they were *responsible* for what happened:

> "There was a certain oracle of those men (the Jews) that the city should be taken and the sanctuary burnt." [This was referring to Daniel's 70 Weeks prophecy, of course.] "When a sedition should invade the Jews and their own hands should pollute the Temple. And they made themselves the instruments of their own accomplishment." **(Josephus)**

In other words, Josephus blamed his own countrymen for the destruction of the Temple. In his mind, the *Jews were the people of the prince who is to come.* And that would mean *Jesus was the prince.* This is a *key understanding.*

## Who Actually Commanded Jerusalem's Destruction?

I suspect that for many of you this realization of exactly who was responsible for the destruction of Jerusalem has come as quite a shock. It's not easy to lay aside notions that have long been part of our Christian upbringing, quite possibly since the earliest days of our faith. But let's consider for a moment that perhaps *God* commanded the destruction of Jerusalem. Now, wouldn't *that* be something!

Let's begin by examining who Jesus prophesied would be the ones to destroy the city of Jerusalem:

> *The king was enraged, and he sent his armies and destroyed those murderers and set their city on fire.* **(Matt 22:7)**

When speaking to the Pharisees in Matt 22, Jesus told the parable of the wedding feast, about how the invited guests (the

Jews) refused to come to the wedding. The invited guests killed and mistreated the king's messengers (the prophets), who had been sent with the wedding invitations. The king became enraged and sent armies to set their city on fire.

So, according to Jesus, it is the King, Yehovah Himself, who sent armies to set the city on fire. *God destroyed the city* using the *Roman armies as His proxies.*

This is confirmed by the equally valid Septuagint Greek text of Dan 9:26:

> *After sixty-two weeks, the anointing [the Messiah] will be destroyed and there will be no Judgment in him and He shall destroy the city and the sanctuary with the leader who is coming.* **(Dan 9:26 LXX)**

This text clearly states that the Messiah will destroy the city in AD 70 with the *leader who is coming.* This was the Roman General Titus.

In AD 70, the unsaved Jews in Jerusalem were living in apostasy, having rejected Jesus as their true Messiah. The Temple supported this apostasy by giving them the mistaken impression that their sins were forgiven through the sacrificial blood of sheep and goats. So if you are wondering why God would authorize the destruction of the city and the Temple, perhaps it was to disrupt the comfortable lifestyle and religious practices of the Jews who had failed to recognize the coming of His Son. Perhaps it was to drive them toward their true Messiah.

We conclude, therefore, that it was God who commanded the destruction of Jerusalem, using Romans, Syrians, and Jews as

His proxies to accomplish His Will. *This is an important insight.* All three of these nationalities are Jesus's people, in a sense. Although Jesus was Jewish and from the tribe of Judah, *all* people are the *people of the prince who is to come* — Jesus: Those saved will come from every tribe and language and people and nation who accept his salvation.

This is probably the best sense of the meaning of Dan 9:26: That the Prince did not destroy the city of Jerusalem directly; rather, those doing His bidding did so. In this way, Dan 9;26 is not a verse about *ethnicity* at all; it is a verse about *agency*.

## Who is the Prince?

We just completed our discussion of the *prince* and *the people* associated with the Destruction of Jerusalem in AD 70. Based on that, perhaps scholars have been looking at Dan 9:26 *backwards*. And, just maybe, instead of working in reverse from Dan 9:27 to figure out who the anonymous *he* was, we should have been working forward from the beginning of the passage to allow the scripture to interpret itself. What a novel idea!

When we move in the *logical* forward direction, scripture tells us *exactly* who the *prince who is to come* will be:

> *From the issuing of a decree to restore and rebuild Jerusalem until Messiah the Prince there will be seven weeks and sixty-two weeks.* **(Dan 9:25)**

Jesus is given two titles: *Messiah and Prince*. He plays both roles. Then, in the very next verse of Daniel, these roles are separated, representing the *two comings* of Jesus. At His First Coming, the Messiah died on the cross. At His Second Coming, He will return as Prince to rule the whole world:

> *The Messiah will be cut off and have nothing, and the people of the prince who is to come will destroy the city and the sanctuary.* **(Dan 9:26)**

Just about everyone misses that. But the Hebrew words for *Messiah* and *Prince* are *identical* in the two verses, Dan 25 and 26. And it is the same person, Jesus, filling two roles. The reason that nearly every scholar misses this interpretation is two-fold. *First*, they fail to realize that God is the one who authorized the destruction of Jerusalem, for His own righteous purposes; and they therefore project this act upon an evil prince. *Second*, they fail to realize that the agents of that destruction — Roman, Syrian, and Jewish — are *all* Jesus's people.

## Impact of This Prophecy

A tremendous amount is at stake with the question which was asked at the beginning of our discussion in this article: *Will the Tribulation begin with a peace plan?* Assuming that it will, or expecting that anyone who signs a peace treaty with Israel will be the Antichrist, are *both* very dangerous assumptions. Wrongly believing these assumptions will almost certainly cause Christians to become complacent in their search for the truth about the beginning of the 70th Week of Daniel and about the identity of the Antichrist, two of the most critical questions in all of eschatology.

Scripture provides one, and only one, clear sign to watch for, and only one way to identify the Antichrist:

> *When you see the abomination of desolation spoken of by the prophet Daniel standing in the holy place.* **(Matt 24:15)**

*That* is the sign all believers are to watch for. And it is the same sign that we see mentioned in Dan 9:27:

> *On the wing of abominations will come one who makes desolate.* **(Dan 9:27)**

This — and only this — will be the revealing of the Antichrist and the sign that marks the beginning of the Great Tribulation. It is the one sign everyone should know and watch for.

Now, before we move on to the next article, let's address just a couple of more points which are crucial to the understanding of the Dan 9:27 prophecy and what it will mean to those living in the end times.

## Jesus Strengthens the Covenant

This article has probably left you with some questions, among which might be this one: If Jesus is the *He* of Dan 9:27, *what Covenant* is it that He makes or strengthens, and why does He do so for *only* seven years? By process of elimination, we know that it can't be the Abrahamic Covenant, because the land-grant aspect of that Covenant only becomes effective after the 70th Week of Daniel. It can't be the Mosaic Covenant, because Jesus's blood has replaced once and for all the need for the blood of sheep and goats. And it can't be the Davidic Covenant, because Jesus will not sit on His Throne on earth until after the 70th Week.

So, by process of elimination, the Covenant that is strengthened *must* be the *New Covenant*, the one which resulted from the sacrifice of His own blood. But how is this possible, and why is it even necessary? Once a person is saved, they are saved. There is no strengthening of this aspect required.

## Will the Tribulation Begin With a Peace Treaty?

The answer is that the New Covenant also involves an *infilling by the Holy Spirit*. This aspect can *definitely* be strengthened. Might the Spirit lavish gifts through this process upon believers during the 70th Week, to assist them in their mission to overcome the Evil One? Might these gifts of the Spirit include such things as the power of healing and the gift of tongues? If demonic activity will increase during this period, doesn't it seem just as likely that God will ramp up the supernatural gifts available to believers — in an Acts 2 manner — in order to counteract this activity? I believe He will.

Matt 10 contains instructions to the twelve apostles, whom Jesus sent out two-by-two. Included in these instructions are direct quotes from Jesus's end times instructions of Matt 24 about the period of the Great Tribulation. He ends this section by saying:

> *You will not finish going through the cities of Israel until the Son of Man comes.* **(Matt 10:23)**

Clearly, the end time aspect of what Jesus said did not apply to the apostles in the first century, so it appears that this must be a *dual fulfillment* passage. Yes, Jesus was speaking to the apostles in the first century, but He was also speaking to believers at the end of the age. If that is true, then this amazing passage will apply to those who enter the 70th Week of Daniel:

> *Heal the sick, raise the dead, cleanse the lepers, cast out demons. Freely you received, freely give.* **(Matt 10:8)**

Will believers raise the dead in Jesus's Name and cast out demons in the 70th Week? I believe they may. I think it is highly likely that Jesus was speaking not only to the apostles, but also to those who will serve Him at the end of the age, as well.

## Jesus Eliminates Jewish Sacrifices at the Midpoint

In Dan 9:27, we also learn that the *He* eliminates Jewish sacrifices at the midpoint of the 70th Week of years. Obviously, Jesus does not do this directly; He authorizes the Antichrist to do it as His agent. This is done in the same way that God commanded the destruction of the Temple in AD 70, which was accomplished by human agents. And the reason for the elimination of sacrifices in the last days will be exactly the same as it was at the time of the destruction of the Temple: Sacrifices of sheep and goats are a *crutch* for the unsaved Jews, giving them the erroneous impression that they have been granted forgiveness for their sins. Eliminating the sacrifices is one more way in which Jesus will cause the unsaved to seek the *one true source* for the forgiveness of sins: The blood of Jesus.

Believing that Dan 9:27 is all about the Antichrist puts our focus in the *wrong place* — on the tormentor, not on the Savior. It causes us to consider that the 70th Week is all about punishment, rather than a time of great heroism and testimony by the Church. But now that the book of Daniel is unsealed, we can better understand the role Christians will play in the great plan which God has ordained for the end of the age.

# Article Nine

## The Prophecy That Satan Feared

Daniel the prophet was given some of the most amazing end times visions. One of the most detailed of these prophecies is Daniel's *Great, Final Vision*, in Dan 10-12. Is this the prophecy Satan feared so much that he tried to keep it secret? And if it is, isn't it the one we should perhaps study most carefully?

Why would Satan fear the prophecy in Dan 10-12 so much? What secrets does it contain that Satan did not want to be known? And how did Satan try to keep this final vision from being released to Daniel? This article will describe one of the greatest examples of spiritual warfare in the Bible and reveal the text that Satan didn't want anyone to see.

The Great, Final Vision wasn't Daniel's first rodeo. In total, Daniel interpreted two dreams for King Nebuchadnezzar; revealed the meaning of the writing on the wall in King Belshazzar's banquet hall; and experienced four of this own visions, which include three found in Dan 7, 8, and 9 and a fourth, final vision, which was found in Dan 10-12. These last four prophetic visions occurred over a period of 17 years. The following table summarizes the four visions of Daniel:

| Vision | Year | Scope |
|---|---|---|
| 4 Beasts | 553 BC | End Times |
| Ram and Goat | 551 BC | End Times |
| 70-7's | 538 BC | Babylon to End Times |
| Great Vision | 536 BC | End Times? |

Figure 9-1

When Daniel received his first vision about the four Beasts, he was confused about what it meant. His thoughts greatly alarmed him, but he kept the vision and this thoughts to himself:

> *As for me, Daniel, my thoughts were greatly alarming me and my face grew pale, but I kept the matter to myself.* **(Dan 7:28)**

When he received the second vision about the Ram and Goat, Daniel became ill for days. This time, he tried to share the vision; but no one could help him understand what it meant. Then 13 years went by, without another recorded vision.

During that intervening period, the fortunes of Israel had changed. The 70 years of exile were about to be completed, and the Jews were anxious to return to Jerusalem. Daniel fell to his knees and asked God's forgiveness for his nation. In response, God gave him the prophecy of the 70-7's, which we examined in part in the previous article.

As Dan 10 begins, Daniel revealed that he has been mourning and seeking the Lord for three weeks:

> *In those days, I, Daniel, had been mourning for three entire weeks. I did not eat any tasty food, nor did meat or wine enter my mouth, nor did I use any ointment until the entire three weeks were completed.* **(Dan 10:2-3)**

Later in the chapter, we learn the reason for this fasting. And we find out from an angel what the results have been:

> *Do not be afraid, Daniel, for from the first day that you set your heart on understanding this and on humbling*

*yourself before your God, your words were heard, and I have come in response to your words.* **(Dan 10:14)**

So, Daniel was fasting and seeking God because he lacked understanding. For 17 years Daniel had longed to understand his previous visions. Now that Israel's captivity was over and the exiles were returning to the land of their ancestors, Daniel must have felt an urgent need to understand the meaning of the visions, so that he could share them with his brethren.

This understanding that Daniel lacked for 17 years was finally granted to him:

*A message was revealed to Daniel, who was named Belteshazzar; and the message was true and one of great conflict, but he understood the message and had an understanding of the vision.* **(Dan 10:1)**

We're going to find out in the next section that Satan went to extreme lengths to try and prevent Daniel from getting this message. And now we know one of the reasons why: This was the capstone to Daniel's other 3 visions. This vision would explain the others and help Daniel (and us) understand the meaning of, and reasons for, the visions. And, as we have seen in previous articles, these visions formed the basis for much of what John recorded in Revelation. So a great deal of our end times information hinged on this prophecy being *understood* by Daniel.

## A Vision of Jesus

After his fast was completed, Daniel was walking with some contemporaries when he saw Jesus in a pre-incarnate, Old Testament appearance. This is recorded in Dan 10:4-6. We know this was Jesus, because it is the same appearance John described in Rev 1:12-16. The similarities between the two passages are striking:

- Daniel saw Jesus dressed in linen; John saw him in a robe.

- Daniel saw his waist girded with gold; John saw him with a golden sash.

- Daniel saw his body like the gemstone beryl; John saw his body like the gemstones jasper and sardius.

- Daniel saw his face like lightning; John saw his face like the sun.

- Daniel saw his eyes like flaming torches; John saw his eyes like fire.

- Daniel saw his feet like burnished bronze; John saw them like metal glowing in a furnace.

- Daniel heard his voice like a tumult; John heard a sound like many waters.

Can there be any doubt that these visions were of the same person? *None at all*. And since John identified this vision as Jesus, we know that this is who Daniel saw, as well.

When Daniel saw the vision, his friends were filled with dread and ran away. Which is exactly the same experience Paul had on the road to Demascus. Paul saw Jesus, and his compatriots were filled with fear. Daniel saw Jesus and did what any red-blooded person would do: He fainted:

> *I retained no strength. But I heard the sound of his words; and as soon as I heard the sound of his words, I fell into a deep sleep.* **(Dan 10:8-9)**

This falling into a *deep sleep* is the identical reaction that John had after seeing his vision of our Lord: John states that he fell at Jesus's feet, like a dead man.

We might well ask why Daniel and John were given the identical vision of Jesus, and why did they have the identical reaction? We can only speculate, but one possible reason is to demonstrate that John's vision in the book of Revelation was intended to further explain Daniel's Great, Final Vision, to certify that they were indeed two visions of the same events.

## Spiritual Warfare

After Daniel had fallen into *deep sleep* (fainted), we come to one of those rare moments in scripture when the veil between the spiritual realm and the physical is drawn back, if only for a moment, to allow us to view the spiritual struggle that was going on.

We then learn from the scripture that the vision of Jesus had departed, and a messenger angel awakened Daniel. What he said was incredible:

> *I have come in response to your words. But the prince of the kingdom of Persia was withstanding me for twenty-one days.* **(Dan 10:12-13)**

The angel tells us that he was being *withheld* by someone known as the *Prince of Persia*. Now no human could hold back an angel sent by God, certainly not for 21 days. What we see referenced here is a supernatural struggle between good angels and bad angels. The fallen angel, the Prince of Persia, was trying to stop Daniel from getting this prophecy. But the archangel Michael came to the rescue of this messenger angel to ensure that the message was delivered to the prophet.

The fallen angel is given a most instructive name. He is called the *Prince of the Kingdom of Persia*. In Hebrew, the word translated as *prince* is *sar*, which is a term frequently applied to *heavenly beings*. It means *captain, commander,* or *general*. In the Septuagint, the Greek word used to describe this fallen angel is *archon*, which is translated *ruler*.

Here are a couple of angelic references from the New Testament that use this word, *archon*:

> *For our struggle is not against flesh and blood, but against the rulers, against the powers, against the world forces of this darkness, against the spiritual forces of wickedness in the heavenly places.* **(Eph 6:12)**
> 
> *But the Pharisees were saying, "He casts out the demons by the ruler of the demons."* **(Matt 9:34)**

Both passages use the term *archon*, which translates as *ruler(s)*, and both passages imply a hierarchy of demonic powers. The evil angel in Dan 10 is one of these ruler angels, and it appears that he is in charge of the nation of Persia. Does Satan assign demonic angels to rule the nations? Clearly, it appears that he does.

Later in the passage we learn that, after the *archon* of Persia, the *archon* of the Kingdom of Greece (Yavan) will arise:

> *I shall now return to fight against the prince of Persia; so I am going forth, and behold, the prince of Greece is about to come.* **(Dan 10:20)**

In addition to the heirarchy of demonic powers, the passage in Dan 10 also implies that there also exists a hierarchy of heavenly angels. Michael is dispatched to help the messenger angel, and he is described as one of the *sar* of the Holy angels — those that didn't fall in Satan's rebellion. Later, in Dan 10:21, we learn that Michael is the *sar* of the Jewish nation of Israel. Because he is listed as only one of the rulers, the passage implies that there are more rulers like him.

Is it possible that the *Sheep* nations of Matt 25:31 have Holy rulers, while the *Goat* nations have demonic rulers? We don't know. It is not explained to us. Maybe all the nations have both. Do the United States, Australia, Britain, South Africa, etc. all have *archon* or *sar* angels? I think that may be possible, if not likely.

## Satan's Dominion

So, how is it that Satan has the authority to assign demons to the various nations? An exchange between Jesus and Satan in Luke provides fascinating insight:

> *He (Satan) led Him (Jesus) up and showed Him all the kingdoms of the world in a moment of time. And the devil said to Him, "I will give You all this domain and its glory; for it has been handed over to me, and I give it to whomever I wish. Therefore if You worship before me, it shall all be Yours." Jesus answered him, "It is written, 'You shall worship the Lord your God and serve Him only."* **(Luke 4:6-7)**

So, we see from this passage that the *earthly domain* and its earthly glory has been *handed over to Satan*, for the time being; and he can give it to whatever human he wishes! In this exchange, Satan tempts Jesus with the kingdoms of the world. But Jesus refused his demand for worship. Someday Satan will give this domain to the *Antichrist*. The Antichrist will be willing to meet Satan's demand for worship and bow down to him.

The earthly domain originally belonged to Adam, but Satan stole it from him in the *fall*. Satan said *it has been handed over to me*. Satan then became the ruler (*archon*) of this world (John 14:30).

## Jesus Will Assume the Dominion

It is believed by many that the scroll with seven seals in the Book of Revelation is the *Title Deed* to the earth, which Jesus shall open during the 70th week of Daniel. After he opens this scroll, Jesus and the saints will rule the earth:

> *But the court will sit for judgment, and his (the Little Horn's) dominion will be taken away, annihilated and destroyed forever. Then the sovereignty, the dominion and the greatness of all the kingdoms under the whole heaven will be given to the people of the saints of the Highest One; His kingdom will be an everlasting kingdom.* **(Dan 7:26-27)**

This concept is poorly understood. Many Christians today believe that Jesus is ruling the earth, *right now*. If you also believe this, please consider this question: "Why do we experience all the wickedness and pain that we do if Jesus is regining?" Jesus *is* seated on a throne, but it is not *His* Throne; it is His Father's Throne. Jesus will remain seated there in heaven until all of His enemies are ready to be subdued:

> *The Lord says to my Lord: "Sit at My right hand until I make Your enemies a footstool for Your feet."* **(Psa 110:1)**

The dominion of the earth *still awaits Jesus* to be proclaimed King and sit upon His own Throne on the earth. This doesn't happen until after the seventh trumpet:

> *Then the seventh angel sounded; and there were loud voices in heaven, saying, "The kingdom of the world has become the kingdom of our Lord and of His Christ; and He will reign forever and ever."* **(Rev 11:16)**

This is the same event, after the seventh trumpet, that is pictured in Daniel:

> *I kept looking in the night visions, And behold, with the clouds of heaven One like a Son of Man was coming, And He came up to the Ancient of Days And was presented before Him. And to Him was given dominion, Glory and a kingdom, That all the peoples, nations and men of every language might serve Him.* **(Dan 7:13-14)**

This passage clearly indicates, as does the passage in Revelation, that the granting of the Kingdom and dominion is an end times event, *after* the opening of the scroll with seven seals.

So why do so many Christians believe that Jesus is ruling the earth right now? Jesus did defeat Satan and his fallen angels at the cross:

> *He made you alive together with Him, having forgiven us all our transgressions, having canceled out the certificate of debt consisting of decrees against us, which was hostile to us; and He has taken it out of the way, having nailed it to the cross. When He had disarmed the rulers and authorities, He made a public display of them, having triumphed over them through Him.* **(Col 2:13-15)**

But that triumph was in regard to the canceling of the certificate of debt, what we owed for our sins. Jesus defeated the law of sin and death by His death on the cross, but the dominion of the earth still awaits Him. He has *not yet* taken control. This is a *key understanding*.

So, although Jesus will rule the earth in the near future, Satan is still ruling; and he is assigning his demonic rulers to the nations. It was one of these demons who tried to stop the messenger angel from bringing the prophecy to Daniel.

## A Prophecy of the End Days

But when the messenger angel was finally able to escape and deliver the message to Daniel, what he said was important:

> *Now I have come to give you an understanding of what will happen to your people in the latter days, for the vision pertains to the days yet future.* **(Dan 10:14)**

The *latter days* that the angel referred to are, literally, the *end days* in Hebrew — the final days. So this message is just as pertinent to us today, because it is still *in the future*. The messenger angel was fighting because he knew that if Daniel didn't get the message, then neither would we.

The wicked angels knew that God does nothing without first telling his prophets (Amos 3:7). We can assume, therefore, that the demons both intended to prevent Daniel from *understanding* the message and, quite possibly, from *hearing it* at all. Perhaps they believed that if Daniel did not hear or understand the message, then it would not come true. That was the nature of this spiritual battle.

The messenger angel also refers to an interesting book, the *Book of Truth*:

> *However, I will tell you what is inscribed in the writing of truth.* **(Dan 10:21)**

What is this book? We know that it's not the scriptures, because at the time of the prophecy none of the events the angel was about to show Daniel had yet been recorded. These were new prophetic events. So the *Book of Truth* must refer to a heavenly edict of what will happen. Psalms seems to also refer to this book:

> *Your eyes have seen my unformed substance; And in Your book were all written The days that were ordained for me, When as yet there was not one of them.* **(Psa 139:16)**

This should encourage us, that God has a plan: No matter what transpires between now and the finality of that plan, no matter how that plan affects us, *God is in control.*

What we do know is this: Satan feared the message which the angel brought to Daniel so much that he tried to prevent its delivery. We know also that the message was possibly meant as further explanation of earlier visions that had confused Daniel and caused him anguish. We learned at the beginning of this section that Daniel understood both the message and the vision after hearing the message, so the angel obviously answered his questions about the earlier visions. This vision may, in fact, be a *key to understanding* the book of Daniel and all of the visions received by Daniel.

When we imagine the invisible war pictured in the following passage from Ephesians, Daniel's 21-day prayer and fasting become even more poignant. Was his prayer and God's empowerment what unlocked the prophecy?

> *Our struggle is not against flesh and blood, but against the rulers, against the powers, against the world forces of this darkness, against the spiritual forces of wickedness in the heavenly places ... pray at all times in the Spirit, and with this in view.* **(Eph 6:12, 18)**

Doesn't it make sense for us to also be in *earnest prayer and fasting* in search of wisdom? Such efforts also teach us to be patient in seeking answers to those prayers. If the messenger angel needed the archangel Michael's assistance to reach Daniel, perhaps we need to understand that the lesser issues facing us may be delayed, as well, by such spiritual forces of darkness. But that should not stop us from praying. God answers our prayers.

In the next article, we will further explore this prophecy, the one that answered Daniel's questions, the one that Satan feared and tried to stop.

# Article Ten

## The Prophecy That Answered Daniel's Questions

God revealed the future to Daniel the prophet in a series of prophecies and dreams throughout his life. But these left him with a great many questions. Finally, when Daniel was older, God provided him with another vision to provide answers to most of Daniel's questions:

> *In the third year of Cyrus, King of Persia, a word was revealed to Daniel, who was named Belteshazzar. And the word was true, and it was a great conflict. And he understood the word and had understanding of the vision.* **(Dan 10:1)**

Never before had Daniel said he understood a vision.

In the last article, we learned that the prophecy in Dan 11-12 — the one that seems to have answered Daniel's questions — is also the one that Satan didn't want anyone to see. As we said earlier, this means we should study it with special interest.

And although *Daniel understood* it, we have not been so fortunate. Quite frankly, we still struggle today to completely comprehend the meaning of this vision. The main question we typically have is this: How much of the prophecy is about the past, and how much is about the future? There are three main theories:

## The Prophecy That Answered Daniel's Questions

1. All of the vision is about the future.

2. About half of it is about the future.

3. Only the final portion is about the future.

Very few prophecies in the Bible are as confusing in terms of their timing. Let me share something that I have found to be true among prophecy teachers who have studied Daniel. Without sharing names, let me just say that — from my personal conversations with a number of them — it appears there is no prophecy in the Bible about which they are more unsure than this one. So don't feel badly if you are unsure about it, as well.

Even so, the answer to the question about *how much* of this prophecy is *yet in the future* is a very, very important one. What verses and events can we rely on to be about the future, and which ones do we know for certain are in the past? Before we tackle that question, let's look at the prophecy from a higher elevation. I divide these two chapters (Dan 11 and 12) into five sections:

1. Material parallel to the Ram and Goat vision.

2. Material about wars and marriages between various Kings of the North and Kings of the South.

3. Material involving a character known as the *despicable* person.

4. Material that is universally thought to apply to the Antichrist.

5. The interpretation of the vision by the messenger angel.

The final two sections are believed by most scholars to apply solely to the future. It is in the first three sections that the controversy about timing is most apparent.

## Material Parallel to the Ram and Goat Vision

In the previous article, we learned that the messenger angel told Daniel that *the vision pertains to the latter days* (Dan 10:14). Literally, in the Hebrew, the angel said the vision pertains to the end of days or the end times.

From this, it would appear that the vision is entirely *in the future*. However, the vast majority of modern scholars claim that the future aspects of the vision don't begin until three-fourths of the way through Dan 11. This is because there is an uncanny resemblance between some of the events detailed in this chapter and actual, historic events. However, as you will soon discover, these events do not match the historic record *perfectly*. This at least implies that there is a possible *dual (near/far) fulfillment* for this prophecy: Some of the events were foreshadowed by historic events, but final fulfillment lies in the future.

The prophecy begins:

> *And now I will show you the truth. Behold, three more kings shall arise in Persia, and a fourth shall be far richer than all of them. And when he has become strong through his riches, he shall stir up all against the kingdom of Greece.* **(Dan 11:2)**

One of the reasons that Daniel was not confused about this prophecy is that the angel doesn't call these kings horns, Goats, or Rams. He clearly numbers the kings and says where they

## The Prophecy That Answered Daniel's Questions

come from. This pattern of clear and detailed explanations continues throughout the prophecy.

But was this verse entirely fulfilled in the past, or does its fulfillment still lie in the future? There is a lot riding on the answer. The knee jerk — yet popular — reaction is to say that it is in the past only. That's easy to do: The passage mentions Cyrus and says four more kings will arise in Persia prior to a king that most assume is Alexander the Great. What could be clearer?

Well, unfortunately for this theory — and for those who look for easy answers — there were more than four kings between Cyrus and Alexander the Great! Many more. In fact, there were 12 more kings: Cambyses II, Bardiya, Darius the Great, Xerxes I, Artaxerxes I, Xerxes II, Darius II, Artaxerxes II, III, IV, Darius III, and Artaxerxes V. Now what?

In the Second Century, during the Jewish *Bar Kokhbah* revolt against Rome, *Rabbi Akiva ben Joseph* (author of the *Mishna*) used this passage as a means of bolstering the messianic credentials of *Simon bar Kokhbah*. Jewish leaders were well aware that the 70 Weeks Prophecy of Dan 9 gave a timetable from the decree to rebuild Jerusalem to the coming of the Messiah. Those 483 years had long since expired during the ministry of Jesus.

So, the resourceful second century Jewish leaders, desperate to bolster *bar Kokhbah*, changed the calendar. They pointed out that there were only *five Persian kings* listed in Dan 11:2. Based on this *evidence*, they claimed that history was wrong and removed 154 years! That would be the equivalent today of saying we were suddenly now living in the 1870's!

Removal of these years from Jewish history allowed Rabbi Akiva to claim that bar Kokhbah fulfilled Daniel's 70 Weeks Prophecy. Obviously, he was mistaken. Moreover, despite Israel's defeat in this revolt, the *missing* 154 years were not replaced and have *remained* a part of Jewish calendars and history ever since.

Modern attempts to claim that secular, historic dating of the reigns of Persian kings are wrong have persisted until today. However, the discovery of Babylonian astronomical diaries containing detailed night-by-night observations of star positions and lunar cycles have proven beyond doubt that there *were 12* kings between Cyrus and Alexander, *not five*, as Dan 11 states.

The number of Persian kings is not the only inaccuracy with history in the passage. We then read about a mighty king that most assume was Alexander the Great:

> *Then a mighty king shall arise, who shall rule with great dominion and do as he wills. And as soon as he has arisen, his kingdom shall be broken and divided toward the four winds of heaven.* **(Dan. 11:3-4)**

But just as we learned in Article Four about Dan 8, Alexander's kingdom was divided into *more than four* sections. It was initially divided into approximately *two dozen*, which eventually coalesced into *five*, and then into *three*. There was *never* a significant length of time when four kingdoms prevailed.

So we have *two* major, historic disconnects in this prophecy that preclude it from being a prophecy of the past only: The number of Persian kings between Cyrus and Alexander, and the number of kingdoms into which Alexander's empire was divided. These are not things we can simply overlook! Either the Bible is wrong

## The Prophecy That Answered Daniel's Questions

(which it *never* is) or we need to consider that this prophecy might be about something other than just the past. Maybe this is a future prophecy. Am I alone in this belief?

Hardly. Let me quote *The Ellicott Bible Commentary*, a highly respected theological resource from the 19th century:

> *The mere similarity which exists between certain things predicted here (Dan 11) and what actually occurred in the times of the Ptolemys is not sufficient to limit the fulfilment of the prophecy to those times, still less to justify the assumption that the section before us is a history of what occurred ... (and it) may be regarded as typical of what will occur before the coming of the Messiah.* **(Charles Ellicott)**

In other words, noted 19th century theologian Charles Ellicott believed the past *only resembles* this prophecy, it *doesn't fulfill* it. He believed *all* of Dan 11-12 is *future* prophecy.

Keil and Delitzsch, authors of the highly respected *Keil and Delitzsch Old Testament Commentary*, agreed with Ellicott:

> *The prophecy does not at all correspond to this (historic) representation. The Angel of the Lord will reveal to Daniel, not what shall happen from the third year of Cyrus to the time of Antiochus, and further to the resurrection of the dead, but, according to the express declaration of Daniel 10:14, what shall happen to his people* הימים באחרית, *i.e., in the Messianic future, because the prophecy relates to this time.* **(Keil and Delitzsch)**

In addition to the agreement of these noted commentators and the testimony of Dan 10:14, there is an amazing *overall correlation* between Dan 8 and Dan 11 — 23 quotes and correlations to be exact. We detailed these for the first time in the book *Revelation Deciphered (2016)*. In Article Four, we established that Dan 8 was future prophecy. This vast number of correlations suggests that *Dan 11 is future*, as well.

So what might this passage mean if it has future implications?

> *Behold, three more kings shall arise in Persia, and a fourth shall be far richer than all of them.* **(Dan 11:2)**

Four modern Persian kings will arise after *something*. Where is modern Persia and what is that *something*? In Article Four, we've already established that modern Persia is Iran. The most significant *something* that occurred in modern Iran was the Iranian Revolution of 1978, which established the modern state.

Since that revolution, there have been two *Supreme Leaders* or Ayatollahs. The current Ayatollah has served 30 years and is quite ill. It is likely a third will take power within a few years. In Article Five, we suggested that a *12th Imam*, or Shia Muslim Messiah, may come out of Iran. Might this man be the fourth *Persian (Iranian)* leader predicted, the one who is rich? Could this portion of the prophecy be fulfilled within the near, foreseeable future? Yes, it could be. These are events we should watch for carefully.

If those events do occur, the next verse (Dan 11:3) matches the events in Dan 8 perfectly. In Articles Four, Five, Six, and Seven, we have indicated that this prophecy involves a war between *Yavan* (a country based in eastern Greece and western Turkey which doesn't yet exist) and Iran — a war which Yavan wins. The Bible tells us that the empire of Yavan will become *exceedingly great*, and *then be divided* into four smaller, weaker nations.

# The Prophecy That Answered Daniel's Questions

## Wars and Arranged Marriages

After this already familiar territory, we enter a section of scripture from Dan 11:5-20, which details the struggles and arranged marriages of the Kings of the North and the Kings of the South. Ellicott, Keil and Delitzsch painstakingly demonstrate how these events somewhat resemble historic struggles between the Seleucid and Ptolemaic empires — but only somewhat. If you are interested in learning in detail why this isn't *perfectly fulfilled* scripture, I refer you to their works.

If this section is future, how long will it be until it is fulfilled? Those who favor the historic interpretation of these verses imagine these events to have occurred over a period of 150 years. But could they happen much, much more quickly — Perhaps in less than ten years? Yes, it's possible. But the timing remains highly speculative.

As we mentioned earlier, there are 23 separate, *exact similarities* between Dan 8 and Dan 11. Yet *not one* of these occurs in the detailed section about struggles and arranged marriages. *Not one.* We're not sure what that means or why this is the one section of the prophecy in Dan 11 that doesn't include similarities with Dan 8.

But if this is indeed future prophecy, Christians will be able to monitor events as they unfold with almost surgical precision — from the division of the Goat into four kingdoms until the time when the Antichrist arises. This is true because, like the first section of the vision, this second section has no symbols. It is clearly and concisely written, with no ambiguity.

## Antiochus or Antichrist

After this last challenging section, we are introduced to a man who is likely the Little Horn:

> *In his place a despicable person will arise, on whom the honor of kingship has not been conferred, but he will come in a time of tranquility and seize the kingdom by intrigue.* **(Dan 11:21)**

Historicists have attributed these verses to the Seleucid King, *Antiochus IV Epiphanes*, who persecuted Israel during the Maccabees period. The sections from Dan 11:21-35 bear an amazing resemblance to the actual career of Antiochus.

But Bible scholar Joel Richardson has shown rather conclusively that these verses and all that follow them are *future prophecy*. It is interesting to follow his logic. Nearly all scholars believe that Dan 12 is future prophecy and involves the time of the Great Tribulation. Richardson noticed that three quotes from Dan. 12 are also found earlier in Dan. 11. This is the Bible's way of indicating that this *is that* — in other words, these *mirror quotes* are the same thing, and from the same period.

Here are the first two *mirror quotes*:

> *Many will be <u>purged, purified and refined</u>.* **Dan 12:11)**

> *Some of those who have insight will fall, in order to <u>refine, purge and make them pure</u>.* **(Dan 11:35)**

This isn't really that controversial. Nearly all scholars believe Dan 11:36 is future prophecy, so this is only one verse earlier than traditional views of Dan 11.

## The Prophecy That Answered Daniel's Questions

Here is the second set of *mirror quotes*:

> <u>Those who have insight</u> will shine brightly like the brightness of the expanse of heaven, and those who <u>lead the many to righteousness</u>, like the stars forever and ever. **(Dan 12:3)**

> <u>Those who have insight</u> among the people <u>will give understanding to the many</u>. **(Dan 11:33)**

The final set of *mirror quotes* involve the Abomination of Desolation:

> From the time that the regular sacrifice is abolished and <u>the abomination of desolation is set up</u>, there will be 1,290 days. **(Dan 12:11)**

> Forces from him will arise, desecrate the sanctuary fortress, and do away with the regular sacrifice. And they will <u>set up the abomination of desolation</u>. **(Dan 11:31)**

Via these 3 sets of *mirror quotes*, Richardson traced the future aspects of the prophecy all the way back to Dan 11:31. Richardson's next step was then to confirm that the character described in verses 31-35 is the same *despicable person* found in Dan 11:21.

This collection of verses — from verse 21 to verse 35 — is a long, continuous passage about a single individual. Therefore, we can be fairly safe in assuming that the Antichrist is the individual found in this passage and onward, until the end of the chapter. Might Antiochus also have fulfilled these passages in some sort of dual fulfillment? Yes, but this section is primarily about the Antichrist.

So let's review what we've learned is future prophecy:

- Dan 11:36 through the end of Dan 12 has always been *assumed to be future* by most scholars.

- We have shown that Dan 11:2-4 *must be future* because these verses are inconsistent with history.

- Joel Richardson has demonstrated that Dan 11:21-35 will be *fulfilled in the future* (even if the section contains a dual historic fulfillment).

The only section about which there is some question as to whether it is future prophecy is the detailed second section about *wars and arranged marriages*. But because it is totally surrounded by other prophetic sections which we now know are in the future, we can *assume* that this section will be fulfilled in the future, as well.

## Future Fulfillment of Dan 11:20-29

Earlier in this article, we analyzed Dan 11:2-4 as if it were future prophecy. Let's now also look at verses 20-29, which have been established as future fulfillment by Richardson. These verses provide amazing detail about the Antichrist's early career, detail not found anywhere else in the Bible:

> *Then in his place one will arise who will send an oppressor (tax collector) through the Jewel of his kingdom; yet within a few days he will be shattered, though not in anger nor in battle. In his place a despicable person will arise.* **(Dan 11:20-21)**

## The Prophecy That Answered Daniel's Questions

This is very interesting. If the *despicable person* is the Antichrist, then he will follow a leader who sends out a tax collector and reigns for only a very short time — for just a matter of days.

We then learn about the despicable person or Antichrist, himself:

> *In his place a despicable person will arise, on whom the honor of kingship has not been conferred, but he will come in a time of tranquility and seize the kingdom by intrigue.* **(Dan 11:21)**

This is a *key verse*. It clearly shows us that the Little Horn, the Antichrist, was not a leader prior to his ascension. Kingship, or *royal majesty* according to some translations, was not given to Little Horn prior to this. This detail — along with other reasons highlighted elsewhere in this book — eliminates most contemporary leaders from consideration to be Antichrist.

We also see that Little Horn obtains the kingdom by *intrigue*. The Hebrew word literally means *smooth or slippery*. It can probably best be translated as *deceit*. Intrigue is definitely the *calling card* of the Antichrist, and it appears that he rises to power in one of the four horns of the Goat using this methodology.

After the Antichrist receives this kingdom, we see that he is challenged militarily, but he overcomes the opposition:

> *The overflowing forces will be flooded away before him and shattered, and also the prince of the covenant.* **(Dan 11:22)**

Who is the *Prince of the Covenant*? We don't know. But perhaps it may refer to an Israeli leader. If so, perhaps Israel feels threatened by the Little Horn at this point and preemptively attacks, is defeated, and retreats. That is our best guess.

We then learn about an alliance that is made by the Little Horn:

> *And from the time that an alliance is made with him he shall act deceitfully, and he shall become strong with a small people.* **(Dan 11:23)**

What kind of Alliance is made? It could be one with Israel or perhaps with other Arab nations. It isn't clear. But again, deceit is how he operates. Could this be the point at which he *plucks out* the other three horns of the Goat by intrigue, as discussed in Articles Five and Six? That is our best guess, because the text says that at this point, he becomes *strong*. This implies he *wasn't strong* until this alliance.

I'm sure many saw the word *alliance*, and immediately concluded this agreement is the *covenant with the many* of Dan. 9:27. But note that the angel specifically avoids using the word *covenant*, choosing instead to use *alliance*. In just the previous verse, an Israeli leader is described using the word *covenant* — as in *Prince of the Covenant* — but that same word is *not* used here.

The Hebrew word which translates as *alliance* is *chabar*. This word is first used in the Bible in a very interesting section of scripture: Abraham's rescue of Lot during the battle of the nine kings. Four of these kings were *joined together* in an alliance. It's that type of association: It's an alliance, *not a peace treaty*.

One of our YouTube Channel's highly astute viewers brought to my attention that the nations of the kings against which Abraham fought in Gen 14 may represent the *four horns of the*

*Goat*. This use of the same Hebrew word for *alliance* in Dan 11 and Gen 14 supports this theory to some degree.

Those nations that joined in the alliance, or *chabar*, represented four of the five sons of Shem, the son of Noah. The four in alliance were Lud, who settled in Turkey; Aram, who settled in Syria; Asshur, who went to Iraq; and Elam, who settled in what is now Iran. These are the *same nations* as the *four horns* of the Goat that we proposed in Article Five. Abraham was a descendent of Arphaxad, the remaining son.

Additionally, this verse we are studying (Dan 11:23), is *amazingly similar* to the verse in Dan 7, about the rising of the little horn:

> *There came up among them another horn, a little one.* **(Dan 7:8)**

> *He shall come up and shall become strong with a small people.* **(Dan. 11:23)**

In both verses, the Little Horn *comes up*, and both verses stress that he is small, or the people he comes from are small. This further reinforces that this passage is speaking of the rise of the Antichrist.

## The Antichrist Expands His Kingdom

The prophecy continues:

> *Without warning he shall come into the richest parts of the province, and he shall do what neither his fathers nor his fathers' fathers have done, scattering among them plunder, spoil, and goods. He shall devise plans against strongholds, but only for a time. And he shall stir up his*

*power and his heart against the king of the south with a great army. And the king of the south shall wage war with an exceedingly great and mighty army.* **(Dan 11:24-25)**

The phrase *without warning* means the Antichrist will be both a man of deception and *suddenness*. But scripture also teaches us that he will be a man who *buys* his loyalty with bribes.

You may remember this map from Article Seven:

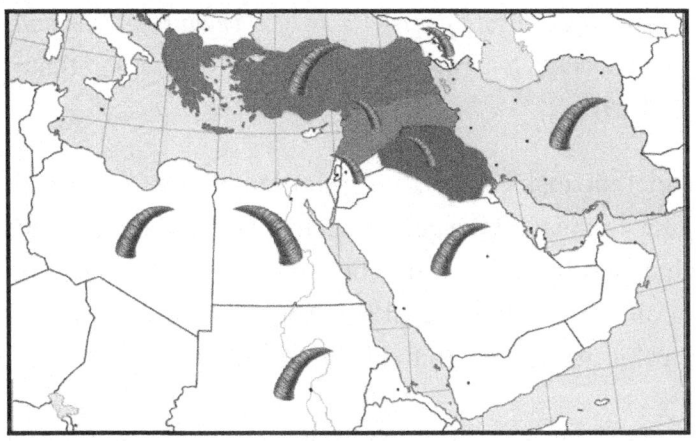

Figure 10-1

The *ten horns* in this theoretical map can be visualized as *five southern* horns and *five northern* horns of the Beast Empire. As we mentioned previously, the southern five horns may be reasonably expected to form an alliance around the individual who becomes King of the South. These five horns will likely include Saudi Arabia, Jordan, Egypt, Sudan, and Libya.

As the prophecy continues, it seems that the King of the South is betrayed by his own generals, those who eat at his table. And the King of the South's army suffers great losses:

## The Prophecy That Answered Daniel's Questions

> *Those who eat his choice food will destroy him, and his army will overflow, but many will fall down slain.* **(Dan 11:26)**

And then we read that the King of the South and King of the North sit down to devise a *peace treaty*; but each lies to the other.

The first half of the 70th Week, then ends on this note about the little horn:

> *He will return to his land with much plunder; but his heart will be set against the holy covenant, and he will take action and then return to his own land.* **(Dan 11:29)**

We read that just before the midpoint of the 70th Week, the Little Horn plans to take action against Israel, the *Holy Covenant*. But what will he do? What action will he take? The Bible isn't clear at all. But we know that the Antichrist takes some form of action as his armies return to his homeland.

In our next article, we'll complete our study of Daniel's prophecies in Dan 11 and 12, and we will discover what the cryptic phrase *time, times, and half a time* may mean.

# Article Eleven

## Time, Times, and Half a Time

What does the cryptic phrase *time, times, and half a time* mean? Sure, we know from previous end times studies that it means approximately 3 ½ years. But why did God choose this phrase about time, and why did He divide it like He did into three segments? In this article we're going to explore this phrase in detail — what it means and what happens during this period, according to the book of Daniel.

Just about every student of prophecy knows that the phrase *time, times, and half a time* means 3 ½ years. But is this all it means? Why did God select this crazy phrase, using the cryptic word *time*? Why didn't He just say 3 ½ years? In other places in Daniel, we see that God uses actual values, like 1,290 days or 1,335 days, which are simple and easy to understand. So, why did God use something so different in this particular prophecy? The answer, like so many others from our study of the book of Daniel, reveals much more than we thought we would ever know.

There are several occurrences of this phrase in both Daniel and Revelation. Let's see what we can find out:

- We first encounter this phrase in Dan 7:25, where we learn that the saints of the Highest One are given into the hands of the Little Horn for this period of time:

    *He will speak out against the Most High and wear down the saints of the Highest One, and he will intend to make alterations in times and in law; and they will be given into his hand for a time, times, and half a time.* **(Dan 7:25)**

- Daniel is told about this phrase once again during his Great, Final Vision in Dan 11-12. And once again it involves the shattering of God's Holy people, the saints.

*It would be for a time, times, and half a time; and as soon as they finish shattering the power of the holy people, all these events will be completed.* **(Dan 12:7)**

- Finally, this phrase is repeated in Revelation. This time, we are told that, after the dragon, who is Satan, is cast out of heaven, he then pursues *the woman*, who is spiritual Israel, or the remnant Israel. But this time provision is made for the saints: And for time, times, and half a time, she is nourished.

*But the two wings of the great eagle were given to the woman, so that she could fly into the wilderness to her place, where she was nourished for a time and times and half a time.* **(Rev 12:14)**

Again, as in the two uses of this phrase in Daniel, this time period represents *a period when the Holy people are persecuted.*

We'll return to all three of these passages shortly and unpack them, but for now let's answer the first question we asked, which was, "Why does God use the cryptic word *time* instead of *year*?"

## What is a *Time*?

And here is our first surprise: The words translated *time* mean *different* things in each of the three passages.

In the first passage, the Aramaic word used is *iddan*, which actually does mean *moment* or *time*. It is used a couple of times in Daniel. In Dan 4, it is used in association with the seven periods of time, or years, during which Nebuchadnezzar's pride caused him to act like a beast. I'm sure most of you recognize that this 7-year period is symbolic of the 7-year 70th Week of Daniel. And, a 3 ½ year period is exactly half of that week of years. But are these our traditional *365-day* years?

I would say *absolutely not*. They are *Hebraic* years, which are different. In the passage in Dan 12, the word translated as *time* changes from the *Aramaic* word, *iddan*, to a *Hebrew* word, *mo'ed*, meaning *appointed time* or *appointed meeting*. Now, we have previously discussed how Daniel's vision in Dan 11-12 answered a lot of his questions. We can be fairly certain that Daniel would have wanted to know what the meaning of the phrase *time, times, and half a time* meant. In this final vision, God didn't use Aramaic; He used Hebrew, a language which Daniel understood intimately. So the meaning of the phrase suddenly became clear to Daniel. It may not be clear to you just yet, but it will be once we examine what this word *mo'ed* means.

The appointed times, or *mo'edim* (the plural of *mo'ed*), of Israel are also known as the *Feasts of the Lord* (Lev 23). There are seven of these in a year, beginning with Passover and ending with the Feast of Tabernacles. The timing of the Feasts is different from year to year, and this difference allowed Daniel to know when the *time, times, and half a time* would begin! The Jewish *secular* year begins on the Feast of Trumpets or Yom Teruah, which is usually during the month of September, while the Jewish *religious* year begins on Nisan 1, the first month of the religious calendar, which is typically in March or April. The cycle of the seven Feasts of the Lord begins on Passover. This is a *key* understanding. If God had used the term *year*, Daniel wouldn't have known when to begin the cycle. Now he knew.

So *time, times, and half a time* isn't some random series of 3 ½ years that can begin at just any time. It is a *specific* length of time: *One series* of all seven Feasts of the Lord, or *mo'edim*, beginning with Passover, and followed by *two complete series* of Feasts, beginning on their respective Passovers, which is then followed by *half of the time* from one Passover to the next. And these are *never* 365-day years.

Surprisingly, the word *mo'edim*, or *appointed times*, is found in the Bible even before the creation of man:

> Then God said, "Let there be lights in the expanse of the heavens to separate the day from the night, and let them be for signs and for seasons (mo'edim) and for days and years." **(Gen 1:14)**

In the very beginning, God set the sun and moon in the heavens to control the days and years and the timing of the appointed times, or Feasts of the Lord.

Therefore, the complex Hebraic calendar controls the length of time between one Passover to the next. Some years, that period of time is 353 days. In other years, it might be 354, 383, or 384 days, depending on lunar cycles and whether or not the year is a leap year. Given this, it's logical to wonder whether *time, times, and half a time* is *exactly* 3 ½ years long and, if so, exactly how long is that? The answer likely is *yes* — that period is 3 ½ years;

however, the number of days in that period *varies*, as we have seen. It's not a precise period of time. So, in most cases, a *year* is not quite what a non-Jew would expect it to be.

Let's look at an example from three Passovers — say from Passover 2026 (April 1) to Passover 2029 (March 30th). During this period, there are 1,090 days — or 2 years, 11 months, and 29 days. The next Hebrew year, however, includes a leap year. So three and a half *times* would be three years, six months, and an *extra* 7 days. So, *some periods* of 3 ½ *times* are *greater* than 3 ½ years, and some are actually less. It depends entirely on the particularities of the Jewish years in question.

As many of you know, scripture contains references to specific numbers of days, including 1,260, 1,290, and 1,335. We'll explore these figures later in this article. But what is actually more important than the number of days is *God's focus* on the *Feasts of the Lord* in terms of the end times. And He lets us know this by using the phrase *time, times, and half a time* — or *mo'ed, mo'edim, and half a mo'ed*. The cycle begins on or near a Passover, the first Feast, in the first month of the Hebraic ceremonial year.

## The Beginning of Time, Times, and Half a Time

The midpoint of the 70th Week of Daniel is marked by the Little Horn's *desecration* of the Jewish Temple, the *elimination* of the Jewish sacrificial offerings, and the *setting up* of the Abomination. We have already determined that this time period begins on or near a Passover. But let's return to Dan 12 for more specific information about this time:

> *It would be for a time, times, and half a time; and as soon as they finish shattering the power of the holy people, all these events will be completed . . . From the time that the*

> *regular sacrifice is abolished and the abomination of desolation is set up, there will be 1,290 days.* **(Dan 12:7, 11)**

We see that the beginning of that time is marked by the *abolishing of the sacrifice* and the setting up of the *Abomination of Desolation*, which likely occurs on or near a Passover. Earlier in this same vision, Daniel identifies this event:

> *Forces from him will arise, desecrate the sanctuary fortress, and do away with the regular sacrifice. And they will set up the abomination of desolation.* **(Dan 11:29-31)**

This event also marks the flight of the Jewish remnant from Israel. Jesus spoke of this in Matthew:

> *Therefore, when you see the abomination of desolation which was spoken of through Daniel the prophet, standing in the holy place (let the reader understand), then those who are in Judea must flee to the mountains.* **(Matt 24:15-16)**

Jesus specifically mentions watching for this event (*when you see*), the Abomination, which Daniel warned us about. Jesus told us that all who are in Judea — which is today's West Bank — must flee to the mountains of Israel. Why are they fleeing?

Jesus is clear that immediately after this event, the Abomination of Desolation, the Great Tribulation will begin. It will be the greatest persecution of Jews and Christians in the history of the world. When we remember the pain, suffering, and loss of life that occurred during the Holocaust, then perhaps we can understand — and put into perspective — the scope of the devastation that is to come. In fact, this passage by Jesus is actually a *mirror quote* from Daniel's vision in Dan 12:

> *But pray that your flight will not be in the winter, or on a Sabbath. For then there will be a great tribulation, such as has <u>not occurred since the beginning of the world until now, nor ever will</u>.* **(Matt 24:20-21)**

> *Now at that time Michael, the great prince who stands guard over the sons of your people, will arise. And there will be a time of distress such as <u>never occurred since there was a nation until that time</u>.* **(Dan 12:1)**

But, as we see, Jesus actually *expanded* on the words used in the vision in Daniel, explaining that the desolation to come will be the worst that *ever will* be. So, even though the angel made it clear to Daniel that the coming time of trouble would be the greatest ever known at *that time*, Jesus took it a step further. Jesus said it will be the greatest time of trouble or persecution *ever, for all time*.

Jesus had more to say about this time in Luke 21, in a passage which was *mirrored* by the vision in Dan 11. Both passages speak of inhabitants falling by the sword and being taken captive:

> *There will be great distress upon the land and wrath to this people; and they will <u>fall by the edge of the sword</u>, and will be <u>led captive</u> into all the nations.* **(Luke 21:23-24)**

> *They will <u>fall by sword</u> and by flame, by <u>captivity</u> and by plunder for many days.* **(Dan 11:33)**

And notice the frequently-overlooked aspect in this next passage from Luke: Jesus calls this period the *times of the Gentiles;* and he uses the exact same Greek word for *appointed times*, just as we have seen in the use of *time, times, and half a time*:

> *Jerusalem will be trampled underfoot by the Gentiles until* ***the times*** *of the Gentiles are fulfilled.* **(Luke 21:24)**

In Revelation, we learn even more about this period. We've already seen that the dragon who is Satan persecutes the woman who gave birth to Jesus, the male child. This woman is spiritual Israel, the Jewish remnant. But God gives two wings of the great eagle to the woman to assist her in escaping. He then nourishes the woman and her child away from the presence of Satan for this same period — *time, times, and half a time*:

> *And when the dragon saw that he was thrown down to the earth, he persecuted the woman who gave birth to the male child. But the two wings of the great eagle were given to the woman, so that she could fly into the wilderness to her place, where she was nourished for a time and times and half a time, from the presence of the serpent.* **(Rev 12:13-14)**

So, what are the two wings of the eagle that God gives to the woman? There are lots of theories about this; but the most logical explanation may be found in Isaiah, where we read about those who mount up with wings like eagles, where they are then given strength to endure. This may be the Bible's picture of God granting the remnant Israel supernatural strength to escape Satan's clutches:

> *He gives strength to the weary, and to him who lacks might He increases power. Though youths grow weary and tired, and vigorous young men stumble badly, yet those who wait for the Lord will gain new strength. They will mount up with wings like eagles. They will run and not get tired, they will walk and not become weary.* **(Isa 40:29-31)**

And where is the woman taken? Into the wilderness, or desert mountains, where there are thousands of small caves in which to hide, much like the ones at Qumran where the Dead Sea scrolls were hidden. God's chosen remnant will one day be hidden away, just like the scrolls, and nourished there. Just like God nourished Elijah.

But while God is protecting His Jewish remnant, Satan turns his fury on the Christians:

> *So the dragon was enraged with the woman, and went off to make war with the rest of her children, who keep the commandments of God and hold to the testimony of Jesus.* **(Rev 12:17)**

This is a *critical understanding* about the period *time, times, and half a time*. Satan attacks the Jews *first*. When the remnant is protected supernaturally, *only then* does he turn his persecution on the Christians. We will come back to this point shortly.

Daniel's *Great, Final Vision* includes Christians and their persecution. They are referred to as *those with insight*. In the following passage, we see that the Little Horn will use smooth, deceptive, words to turn the world to godlessness. But those with insight, the *Christians*, will display strength; and they will act in opposition to Little Horn. They won't hide in bunkers or caves. Rather, they will offer testimony and understanding of the Gospel *to the many*:

> *By smooth words he will turn to godlessness those who act wickedly toward the covenant, but the people who know their God will display strength and take action. Those who have insight among the people will give understanding to the many.* **(Dan 11:32-33)**

In the process, many will fall. But Daniel's vision says that they will be resurrected, to shine like stars forever. We know this will be true of those who inherit resurrection bodies:

> *Those who have insight will shine brightly like the brightness of the expanse of heaven, and those who lead the many to righteousness, like the stars forever and ever.* **(Dan 12:3)**

## Four Things the Little Horn Accomplishes

In Dan 7:25 we learned that the Little Horn *wears out* the saints; and they are *given into his hand* for *time, times, and half a time*. According to the following verse, Little Horn accomplishes *three other* things during this time period:

> *He will speak out against the Most High and wear down the saints of the Highest One, and he will intend to make alterations in times and in law; and they will be given into his hand for a time, times, and half a time.* **(Dan 7:25)**

We see that one of his accomplishments is that he *speaks out* against the Most High:

> *He will exalt and magnify himself above every god and will speak monstrous things against the God of gods.*
> **(Dan 11:36)**

He will say monstrous things against Yehovah and against Jesus — and he will glorify himself:

> *He will show no regard for the gods of his fathers or for the desire of women, nor will he show regard for any other god; for he will magnify himself above them all Instead he will honor a god of fortresses, a god whom his fathers did not know; he will honor him with gold, silver, costly stones and treasures. He will take action against the strongest of fortresses with the help of a foreign god.*
> **(Dan 11:37-39)**

Not only will he show no regard for the great God, Yehovah, but he shows no regard for other gods, not even for the gods of the region where he was born.

Additionally, nestled in the phrase about not regarding gods, is a little-understood phrase about not regarding the *desire of women*. What does that mean? Many have taken it to mean that Little Horn will be a homosexual. But why place that information in this section about his lack of regard for gods?

It seems much more likely that this phrase refers to a god of some sort, possible the Babylonian deity *Tammuz*, who was known as *the desire of women*. It is also possible that it refers to the true God, our Messiah, because it was the desire of all Jewish women to bear the Messiah and to be His mother.

The scriptures also tell us who Little Horn will honor: A foreign god, a god of fortresses. Nimrod tried to build the ultimate fortress, the Tower of Babel, in defiance of the true God, and in defense of another worldwide flood. So, I believe this passage may be referring to the demon who will possess the Little Horn. It may be the same demon that possessed Nimrod. Notice that it is a god his fathers did not know; that is because this demon will have just come up out of the abyss. No one on the earth will know him at that point.

In Dan 7:25 we are also informed that Little Horn will try to make alterations in the law and the seasons. What law does he attempt to change? God's Holy law, most certainly! He may even try to substitute Sharia Law.

But what about altering *seasons*? In Aramaic, the word *zeman* means *appointed times*, just as *mo'ed* does in Hebrew. Just how important are the appointed times to the end times? They are among several, primary *things* that the Little Horn attacks: God, God's people, God's law, and the appointed times. I'm sure that's a shock to most Christians, many of whom aren't even familiar with the Feasts of the Lord, the appointed times (Lev 23).

## Daniel's Mysterious Days

Let's look at a couple of alternative theories regarding the mysterious number of days in Daniel and Revelation: 1,260 days; 1,290 days; and 1,335 days. The Bible isn't completely clear what these days are. But if we do some simple math, we discover some interesting possibilities.

In the final chapter of Daniel, *time, times, and half a time* seems to be associated with 1,290 days.

## Daniel Unsealed

> *From the time that the regular sacrifice is abolished and the abomination of desolation is set up, there will be 1,290 days.* **(Dan 12:11)**

What exactly happens at the end of the 1,290 days is not clear from this passage. But let's present a scenario. Let's consider what the outcome would be if the regular sacrifice was eliminated and the Abomination of Desolation was set up on Nisan 1 — the beginning of the Jewish ceremonial year. If we count 1,290 days from this date, where would we end up?

In some Hebraic years, we would conclude counting exactly on the final day of the Feast of Tabernacles. For instance, on the last day of Tabernacles in the Gregorian year 2030, this count is *exactly* 1,290 days. This is quite interesting, because the seventh day of Tabernacles in this example concludes *all* of the *mo'edim*, or Feasts of the Lord, for the year.

The Feast of Tabernacles is also prophetically interesting, for a number of reasons. It is symbolic of God setting up his Tabernacle with man. It is a seven-day Feast, and some believe it is prophetic of the coming Wedding Feast of the Lamb. The day *after* Tabernacles is sometimes known as the Eighth Day, or the Last Great Day. Prophetically, many believe it represents the coming of a new age. Might this be the beginning of the Millennial Kingdom? Perhaps.

But 1,290 days is *not the only* number given in the book of Daniel. It also mentions 1,335 days — 45 days more than 1,290. Adding 45 days to the final day of Tabernacles yields nothing of interest; it's the 6th of Kislev — a normal day, without spiritual significance, two and a half weeks prior to Hanukkah. So, although the 1,290 days fits perfectly, the 1,335 days does not, at least not this example. And all the days need to fit.

## Time, Times, and Half a Time

If we examine the book of Revelation, a different number of days is suggested for *time, times, and half a time*: 1,260 days. In Rev 12, two passages mention the time that the woman is nourished (Rev 12:6 and Rev 12:14):

> Then <u>the woman fled into the wilderness</u> where she had a place prepared by God, so that there she would be nourished for <u>one thousand two hundred and sixty</u> days. **(Rev 12:6)**

> But the two wings of the great eagle were given to the <u>woman</u>, so that she could fly <u>into the wilderness</u> to her place, where she was nourished for a <u>time and times and half a time</u>, from the presence of the serpent. **(Rev 12:14)**

Notice that these two verses — which report the same events — differ only in the manner in which they represent time. It would seem that that we are meant to equate *time, times, and half a time* with *1,260 days* and *not* with 1,290 days.

There is also an interesting relationship between 1,260 days and 1,335 days — a difference of 75 days. If the 1,260 days of *time, times, and half a time* were to end on Yom Kippur, the day of Atonement, in most years the 1,335th day would be Hanukkah, the Feast of Rededication, which honors the rededication of the Temple following the return to Jerusalem. This is either by design, or it is a great coincidence.

But what about the 1,290th day in this scenario? Interestingly, in this scenario the 1,290th day falls on a minor Jewish festival commemorating the day God closed the door of Noah's Ark. Might this be the day of the Sheep and Goat judgment? On that day, God decides who is allowed to enter the Kingdom (the sheep) and who is swept away into the Lake of Fire (the goats).

This is certainly similar to the judgement rendered during the time of Noah. It would also be, appropriately, the end of all rebellion.

In our scenario, all of the days — 1,260; 1,290; and 1,335 — are found to fall on significant Jewish Feast dates on God's calendar, and all occur in exactly the correct order. This relationship between end dates is the same in most years.

But what would be the starting date in this scenario? That has to fit, as well. An analysis of the possible start dates range from four days after Passover in some years to seven days after Passover in others.

Within this range are some very interesting possibilities. One is Nisan 21, which is the date on which the sea was split in Exodus. This might be a date symbolic of God's supernatural protection of the Jews as they run from the forces of evil. In Rev 12:16, we learn of a similar instance. In this case, the ground supernaturally swallows a flood while protecting the *woman*, the Jewish remnant.

In other years, the 1,260-day countdown begins on the day after First Fruits, the day when Jews begin *counting the Omer*. This is a countdown until Pentecost or Shavuot:

> *You shall also count for yourselves from the day after the sabbath, from the day when you brought in the sheaf of the wave offering; there shall be seven complete sabbaths. You shall count fifty days to the day after the seventh sabbath.* **(Lev 23:15-16)**

This is a very interesting possibility for the beginning of the 1,260-day countdown, because it involves *actually counting* the days, which is exactly what would be required in counting 1,260 days until Yom Kippur (Day of Atonement).

In the year of Jesus's Ascension, this counting was literally a *countdown* until the coming of the Holy Spirit, which obviously occurred that year on Pentecost. This is *exactly* what will happen in the end times when the Jews are saved at the Second Coming and receive the Holy Spirit, except that it will occur on the Day of Atonement.

In this scenario, then, I think we have very satisfactory starting and ending dates for *time, times, and half a time*, all with significant prophetic meaning. Is this the answer to the mystery days of Daniel and Revelation? Perhaps. The Bible does not make this clear, but this is a distinct possibility.

## 2,300 Days

This brings up another cryptic number of days found in Dan 8. The prophet overhears two angels discussing *how long* the vision concerning the sacrifices and the Abomination of Desolation would last:

> *Then I heard a holy one speaking, and another holy one said to that particular one who was speaking, "How long will the vision about the regular sacrifice apply, while the transgression causes horror, so as to allow both the holy place and the host to be trampled?" He said to me, "For 2,300 evenings and mornings; then the holy place will be properly restored."* **(Dan 8:13-14)**

This verse provides a timeline to the restoration of the Temple. But it *remains cryptic* for two reasons:

1. First, the length of time mentioned can be interpreted two ways. Jews celebrated an evening sacrifice and a morning sacrifice each day. So 2,300 *evenings and mornings* might be considered 2,300 sets of these sacrifices (or days). On the other hand, they might be considered just 1,150 days, which would be the case if each morning and evening is counted separately. Noted Old Testament scholar C.F. Keil believes that ancient Hebrews would *only* have understood the phrase *evenings and mornings* to mean *single* days. This would be the same understanding we find with Noah's flood, during which the rain fell for 40 days and 40 nights — which of course was only 40 days, not 80 days.

2. A second reason the verse remains cryptic concerns the determination of when the day count of the prophetic period should begin. Should it begin at the *initiation* of the sacrifice, or upon the *removal* of the sacrifice? I don't believe we can be certain based solely on the language of the prophecy. Are there two things being considered here or three? The angel may be discussing three events:

- The regular burnt offering (its initiation)
- The Abomination of Desolation
- The trampling of the Holy Place

If the angel is applying the 2,300 days to these three things, then the beginning of the countdown would be the *initiation* of sacrifices; and we may have an approximate date for the beginning of sacrifices during Daniel's 70th Week. If that is so, it would explain why this number of days is different, and larger, than others found in scripture — like 1,260, 1,290 and 1,335 days. Twenty-three hundred days is approximately six years, which would mean that sacrifices could begin about a year after the 7-year 70th Week of Daniel begins. We don't feel strongly about this timing, but it is a possibility.

The second possibility is that the 2,300 days begin at the Abomination of Desolation and extend well beyond the end of the 70th Week of Daniel. Perhaps the terminal point — nearly 3 years after the end of the 70th Week — represents the building of a new *fourth Temple* by the Lord Jesus Himself.

## Three Divisions of *Time*

This brings us to the *great mystery:* Why did God mention *three* divisions of *time* for *time, times, and half a time*? Why did He divide the period into an approximate one-year period, a two-year period, and a half-year period? Let me give you my thoughts first, and then we'll unpack each idea.

I believe that the *first* division is the persecution of the Jews, the *second* is the time when Satan turns his attention to the Christians and persecutes them, and the *third* division is the wrath of God. Let's look at each division.

As we have already learned, the Beast begins his persecution with the Jews:

> *And when the dragon saw that he was thrown down to the earth, he persecuted the woman.* **(Rev 12:13)**

This likely starts after Passover, 3 ½ years prior to the end. In my opinion, this period of Jewish persecution is the *half a time*, a half-year period during which the full force of the Antichrist and his regime are aimed at Jerusalem and the Jews. It will be a time when he kills many and imprisons the rest — except the remnant that escapes.

The escape of the remnant will infuriate him, and he will turn his fury on Christians. This assault against believers may last two years, in my opinion. As Daniel tells us, many with *insight* (Christians) will fall by sword and captivity. This would represent the *times* of *time, times, and half a time*.

Then, one year before the end, God rescues believers via the rapture and begins to pour out his wrath on the unrepentant.

In my opinion, the various components of *time, times, and half a time* are in *reverse order*: The *half a time*, the persecution of the Jews, comes first; then *times*, the two-year persecution of the Church, comes second; and lastly comes *time*, the one-year period of God's wrath, which is poured out on the unrepentant.

What exactly makes me think that the three time periods might be in reverse order? And why do we think the wrath of God is only one year long? These two concepts are related. The one-year period of wrath is the time we are most convinced about. Applying logic and the process of elimination, we determined the other two time periods.

Let's look at the concept that the wrath of God is about one year in length, which means that Christians likely will not endure all of *time, times, and half a time*. A complete discussion of this subject is quite complex and would require much more space than is possible here. If you wish to look more fully into the details, we refer you to our recently published book, *Dawn of a New Day: The Timing of Christ's Return and Why it Matters*:

Figure 11-1

In Articles Twelve and Twenty of *Dawn of a New Day*, we explain these matters in great detail. Here, however, we will unpack these ideas and give you the abbreviated version.

To begin with, Jesus Himself limited the duration of the persecution of Christians — the elect of the New Testament. In Matt 24:22 Jesus said, *for the sake of the elect, those days will be cut short*. We believe this verse means exactly what it says: That those days of persecution during the Great Tribulation will be cut short for Christians, and *only* for Christians.

The first problem we encounter with this thinking is this: How can the saints be given into the hands of the Little Horn for *time, times, and half a time*, per Dan 7:25, and yet have those days cut short? The answer is actually quite simple: Because those days are not cut short for *everyone*. They are cut short *only* for the *Christian saints*, the elect of the New Testament. The Jewish remnant, some of whom will *eventually* come to faith, are persecuted for the *entire* period of approximately 3 ½ years. For the unsaved Jews, Jesus didn't cut short this period of *time, times, and half a time*. Which means that the Great Tribulation and *time, times, and half a time* are *not* the same. That's right, *they are not the same*.

The period of *time, times, and half a time* is either 1,260 or 1,290 days long. Scripture is reasonably clear on this. But the Great Tribulation — *those days* per the scripture — is what Jesus said will be cut short for Christians. The term *Great Tribulation* is *never* associated with a specific number of days, nor is it *ever* associated with the terms *time, times, and half a time* or *Jacob's Trouble* (Jer 30:7). Christian scholars have long-assumed that these terms mean the same thing as the Great Tribulation, but *nowhere* in scripture is this confirmed. It is an assumption; and it is a bad assumption.

When Jesus used the term *great tribulation* in Matthew, he didn't refer to it as a *specific* time or length of time. He simply said *there will be great tribulation* (Matt 24:21), and that those days of tribulation *will be cut short* for the elect (Matt 24:22).

I realize that this is not what you may have been taught; but scripture makes clear that the Great Tribulation is *only a subset* of *time, times, and half a time*. The whole period is comprised of two parts: The Great Tribulation, and the wrath of God. Together, these parts make up the whole of approximately 3 ½ years. Breaking this down, we find the second part, the wrath of God, to be approximately one year long. By simple math, the Great Tribulation must then be approximately 2 ½ years in length.

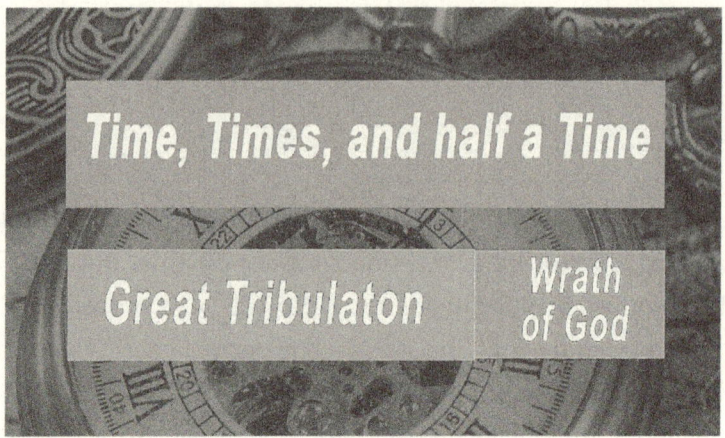

Figure 11-2

So where did the one year period for the wrath of God come from? Consider this verse from Isaiah:

> *For the Lord has a day of vengeance, a year of recompense for the cause of Zion.* **(Isa 34:8)**

Isaiah indicates that the wrath of God begins on His Day of Vengeance, the Day of the Lord; but the recompense, or payback, lasts a year. There are two other verses in Isaiah— Isa 61:2 and Isa 63:4 — that equate the Day of Vengeance with a one-year period.

Additionally, the 70th Week of Daniel is *not* just a simple collection of seven years. Rather, it is a traditional Hebraic *shabua*, or sabbatical cycle. The final year of that sabbatical cycle is set aside for the Lord. Historically, Jews are told to till and harvest the land for six years, and then they are to rest in the seventh year.

The 70th Week of Daniel will be exactly the same: God's people, the Christians, will toil for six years, consisting of 3 ½ years of *birth pangs and* 2 ½ years of the *Great Tribulation*. They will then rest in Heaven during the final year, while God punishes the earth's unrepentant during His wrath.

We find, too, that the flood of Genesis, the first expression of God's wrath, lasted approximately one year. For all of these reasons, and for others discussed in the aforementioned book, we believe that a time period of one year seems the most likely length for the wrath of God.

## Daniel and the Resurrection

This brings us to what is probably the most stunning aspect of Daniel's prophecy: The Resurrection. Daniel was almost certainly aware of Isaiah's prophecy regarding the Resurrection:

> *But your dead will live, Lord; their bodies will rise; let those who dwell in the dust wake up and shout for joy; your dew is like the dew of the morning the earth will give birth to her dead.* **(Isa 26:19)**

But now God gave Daniel his own vision of this same event, and it provided a rough approximation of the timing of that Resurrection:

> *There will be a time of distress such as never occurred since there was a nation until that time; and at that time your people, everyone who is found written in the book, will be rescued. Many of those who sleep in the dust of the ground will awake, these to everlasting life.* **(Dan 12:1-2)**

This event will occur at *that time*, at the time of the Great Tribulation.

Despite the angel's presence, these things remained confusing to Daniel; and the angel explained that they would remain unclear because the words were *sealed* until the end time. Even the prophet Daniel was *not allowed* to completely understand them.

The angel, however, offered hope. The angel said that in the end time, those with *insight* would understand them:

> *These words are concealed and sealed until the end time. Many will be purged, purified and refined, but the wicked will act wickedly; and none of the wicked will understand, but those who have insight will understand.* **(Dan 12:9-10)**

Those with *insight* are you, my brothers and sisters. We are now, finally understanding the formerly-sealed words. And although Daniel could not understand the meaning in his day, the angel reassured him that he would be part of the coming Resurrection:

> *But as for you, go your way to the end; then you will enter into rest and rise again for your allotted portion at the end of the age.* **(Dan 12:13)**

Daniel was reassured that he would be part of the final Resurrection. Historically, this is all anyone who has lived prior to the end times has needed to know. Christians should have been generally satisfied just to be part of the Resurrection, and the details have remained largely unimportant to them. Through the years, even the great reformers and famous theologians struggled with the meaning of the words. But in the end, they, too, didn't need — nor were they able — to understand the words. Just like Daniel, they needed only to know that they would be Resurrected.

But now, it's time that we need to know more. Much more. The book of Daniel has been unsealed, and we have been given knowledge of the words. But more than that, we *need to know their meaning* — because many of us may live to see them fulfilled!

Long ago, on the Mount of Olives, just a couple days prior to His betrayal, Jesus was asked by the disciples about that final phrase from the last verse of Daniel, about *the end of the age*. They asked:

> *Tell us, when will these things happen, and what will be the sign of Your coming, and of the end of the age?* **(Matt 24:3)**

With his response, Jesus began the long process of unsealing the book of Daniel — for them, and for us.

## Article Twelve

## Iron and Clay Mixed

The great metal statue in Nebuchadnezzar's dream included five sections: Four metals and a section of *iron mixed with clay*. What does this final section, iron with clay mixed, mean? This question has confounded scholars since the inception of the Church. There are nearly as many theories about what this means as there are scholars to discuss it:

- Some consider this to indicate a mixture of Church and state — for example, the government of Rome mixed with the papacy.

- Some consider it to be a mixture of two different ethnic groups — like Sunni and Shia Muslims.

- Others consider that this verse may be otherworldly, perhaps representing a genetic combining of men and angels.

- There are those who believe this verse refers to the genetic manipulation of the human genome.

- Some consider that this might foretell a mixing of man and machine, something akin to a cyborg.

- Still others understand the iron to be a microchip, while the clay represents human flesh, leading them to conclude that this portion of the statue represents a futuristic tracking potential.

## Iron and Clay Mixed

In this article we clearly have some exciting — and diverse — subjects to discuss. All of which are implied by the materials found in the feet and toes of this statue, which was revealed in a dream to King Nebuchadnezzar and interpreted by the prophet Daniel:

> *The head of that statue was made of fine gold, its breast and its arms of silver, its belly and its thighs of bronze, its legs of iron, its feet partly of iron and partly of clay.* **(Dan 2:32-33)**

Let's begin with what scripture says about the feet and toes. God's Word clearly defines the statue as five layers:

1. The head of that statue was made of fine gold.

2. Its breast and its arms were silver.

3. Its belly and its thighs were bronze.

4. Its legs were made of iron.

5. Its feet were partly of iron and partly of clay.

When the statue is destroyed by a giant stone, God's Word says that it struck at the feet, not on other parts of the statue. However, as we learn from scripture, the toppled statue crushed all five materials *at once*. Clearly, the statue was supported by the feet; and when it fell, the entire statue was demolished. *All five materials were destroyed.* This is interesting, and we will discuss it later in this article.

Let's look at the prophecy from high elevation:

## Daniel Unsealed

*In that you saw the feet and toes, partly of potter's clay and partly of iron, it will be a divided kingdom.* **(Dan 2:41)**

Daniel's prophecy tells us that the *fifth* kingdom, represented by the feet and toes, will be a *divided kingdom*. Some of it will be strong and some brittle, as represented by the iron and the clay. We could also say that the kingdom is divided into *iron* and *pottery*, as we will discover. So our next task is to figure out what these two terms mean in context.

We know that *iron* is what makes up the *fourth* kingdom. In one of our previous articles, we established that the fourth kingdom was most likely the Islamic Caliphate. But what of the potter's clay? Is it also a kingdom? All of the other materials representing kingdoms are metals; this new material at the foot of the status is not. It is *very* different from the rest of the statue. So different that it could not be there by mistake.

Bible scholar Joel Richardson has suggested that the two elements comprising the feet and toes — the iron and clay — represent the division of the Islamic Caliphate into the principal sects of the Muslim religion: Sunni and Shia. These two sects are in bitter opposition to each other. Richardson has even discussed how the word *mixed* in the scripture — as in *mixed* with iron and clay— is derived from the Aramaic word *arab*, which is often applied when discussing Arab populations, because they are a *mixed* people.

Now, I greatly respect Richardson; and his work on the study of the prophet Daniel may have marked the beginning of its unsealing. But I question this part of his theory. The clay only appears in the final portion of the statue, in the feet and toes, at the *end* of the iron kingdom. But the divide between Sunni and

## Iron and Clay Mixed

Shia has existed from the death of Mohammed onward. It *never* made the Caliphates brittle or breakable. Quite the contrary, the Caliphates ruled the land of Nebuchadnezzar for over 1,400 years.

Richardson's theory also requires that the Sunni and Shia sects be designated as *either* iron or clay, one or the other. But, whereas the difference in tensile strength between iron and clay is clearly *significant*, the difference in power and influence between the two Muslim sects is nowhere near as marked. So for both of these reasons, I'm not a fan of the Sunni-Shia theory proposed by Richardson.

Let's look at another possibility. In Daniel we find that the substance is not just clay, but *potter's clay*. Is there some group of people that might be referred to as potter's clay? If we look to Isaiah, the answer seems obvious:

> *But now, O Lord, You are our Father, We are the clay, and You our potter; And all of us are the work of Your hand.* **(Isa 64:8)**

It's *all of us*! All of us are the work of His hand: As the Bible tells us, He is the potter, and we are the clay. Now, what political entity represents all of us, at least in theory? Why, it's the *United Nations*!

Have you ever heard of the OIC, the Organization of Islamic Cooperation? Fifty-seven nations belong to this voting block within the UN — nearly one-third of the entire United Nations. So Islamic countries already command an inordinate amount of power within the UN.

Ten years ago, non-binding, anti-blasphemy proposals were easily passed in the UN. And although attempts to make them binding on all nations failed at that time, times are changing. Will the coming Caliphate gain in strength and eventually be able to control or manipulate the United Nations? That is a very real possibility. But how exactly might this association between the UN and the Caliphate come to be?

In earlier articles we have written extensively about the break-up of the Goat kingdom into four separate horns, representing four smaller kingdoms. So, who actually does this? Who forces the break-up? As we have previously discussed, in our view it is almost certainly the UN and/or the combined forces of the global super powers. Who else would have the power to do so?

We have also suggested that this breakup of the Goat is the likely time when the 10 horns are set up, as well. If this is true, is the United Nations then somehow initially involved in the governance or oversight of the 10 horns, via some form of alliance? Quite possibly. It may be that the nations of the world will find this necessary as a way to monitor and control the expanding Islamic influence.

I expect that the UN and the world at large will initially fail to understand the significance of this association and with whom they are dealing. The Little Horn will be a master of intrigue and deception, and the United Nations will likely be his playground. Perhaps he will eventually rise to the level of the Secretary-General of the UN. This seems a perfect place from which to expand his world-wide agenda. And although his power will be significant and his use of supernatural forces will enable him to achieve great military victories, he may find that, in some ways, the economic and political power structure of the UN will serve his purposes just as well.

The 10 horns will be strong and brutal, like iron. But the non-Islamic nations of the UN may make any alliance between the UN and the Caliphate as brittle and breakable as pottery. I think this aspect of the prophecy fits perfectly with the prospects for the future. What we will almost certainly see is a fragile, divided alliance, with the Islamic Caliphate dealing from a position of strength.

**The Seed of Men**

There is yet another part to this passage that we need to look at. It is the most controversial part:

> *You saw the iron mixed with common clay, they will combine with one another in the seed of men; but they will not adhere to one another, even as iron does not combine with pottery.* **(Dan 2:43)**

What exactly does *combine with one another in the seed of men* mean? Frankly, there are a hundred ideas; and some are pretty supernatural, including those having to do with hybrids, cyborgs, and Nephilim. But let's take a step back, before we jump to too many conclusions.

I think we can safely say that *the seed of men* definitely involves human procreation or genomes. Let's look at the whole sentence that this comes from. As we see above, the scripture says that *they will not adhere to one another, even as iron does not adhere to pottery*. In other words, the combining is not successful. This is the *key part* of the verse. But what does it have to do with the seed of men?

I think this has to do with an old concept, not a new one; I think it's all about *marriage*. I believe scripture is telling us that marriages between the two groups — iron and clay — won't work. They won't cleave together. Though they combine in the seed of men, the union will not adhere. The iron and the clay will *not become one people*.

Numerous studies by the Pew Group, and others, have revealed that a large percentage of Muslim emigrants to non-Muslim countries do *not* assimilate well. Rather, they retain their distinctive Islamic culture. This is precisely the meaning of *not adhere*. There is very little cleaving, even in marriages, between iron and clay.

You may find it interesting that, even in the Bible, not all arranged marriages worked out. Here are a couple of examples from scripture related to the end times:

- In the distinctive prophecy of Dan 11 we find a passage in which the daughter of one king is brought to another king. But instead of a happy union, we find that *she will be given up*. In other words, the marriage won't cleave.

- In another passage in Dan 11 we find a similar arrangement that does not go so well, where *she will not take a stand for him or be on his side*. Again, there is no cleaving.

In my opinion, what we have in Dan 2:43 is a situation in which two distinct peoples are unable to become *one people*. There is no joining, no cleaving, no assimilation. They may exist in the same space, but they are not one people and do not share a common interest.

## Iron and Clay Mixed

But what about the cyborgs and the Nephilim? Let's start with the Nephilim theory. In Gen 6:4 we find a small, tantalizing verse that presents the concept of the Nephilim. The non-canonical book of Enoch supports the idea that the Nephilim were hybrids of fallen angels and humans. The Nephilim theory of the end times holds that when Satan's fallen angels are cast out of heaven during the 70$^{th}$ Week, this same type of inter-breeding of angels and humans will take place.

Now, I believe that the end times will witness horrible demonic activities following the fall of Satan. But is Dan 2:43 really talking about a physical association between humans and fallen angels? Let's look at the verse and see why some claim it is.

Those who favor this theory focus on the segment of the verse which says that *they will combine with one another in the seed of men.* They then ask, "Who is *they*?" Their conclusion is that *they* must mean angels. I'm sorry, but this is a terrible example of taking a verse out of context.

When we look at the entire verse, we find that *they* means the two elements, the *iron and clay*. We have already defined these things. Iron is a kingdom, *not* angels. And clay is *all people*, who are the work of God, the Potter. Angels are *not* found in this verse. Could the sins of Noah's day and the situation recorded in Gen 6:4 be repeated in the future? Quite possibly. But Dan 2:43 is not the place.

This same process can be used to dispute the claims of those who believe Dan 2:43 is all about genetic manipulation and cyborgs. Although we see evidence of these things in our lives today — and they very well may happen to a greater degree in the future — this verse isn't in reference to that. Instead, Dan 2:43 is about two peoples who try to combine into one but don't adhere or mix. When we evaluate scripture, we need to avoid manipulating verses in an effort to make the Bible say more than it really does.

I suspect that some of these exotic theories are possible, even likely. For instance, when we find in scripture, in Rev 13:15, that the false prophet causes earth dwellers to make an image of the Beast that breathes and talks, this sounds a lot like a cyborg to me. But our specific verse, Dan. 2:43 — about mixing iron and clay — isn't about that. So, although we may find application of some theories in the text of scripture, we should be careful about jumping to conclusions.

## Destruction of the Statue

You will recall from earlier our description of the destruction of Nebuchadnezzar's stature, which included the *simultaneous* break-up of *all five materials at the same time*. And they were destroyed *without a trace*. In a previous article we contrasted this with the four Beasts of Dan 7, in which the terrifying Beast was killed, but the other three beasts were allowed to *live on* for a period of time. So, for those who continue to maintain that the statue of Nebuchadnezzar's dream in Dan 2 and the four Beasts of Dan 7 are the same, this clearly shows that they are *not*. *Everything* within the statue is destroyed *at the same time*.

But how does this happen? How could Babylon be destroyed at the same time as the final kingdom of iron and clay? Wasn't Babylon destroyed long before, along with Persia and all of the other ancient kingdoms? Well, yes and no.

The various governments controlling the land that once belonged to King Nebuchadnezzar's Babylon have been *continuous* since those days. They are *one statue*. This statue

## Iron and Clay Mixed

contains elements of each ruling entity, from then until now. Elements of the Babylonian state still exist today, as do elements of Persia and of the other ancient kingdoms. But the *stone that is Jesus* will strike the end times portion of the statue (the feet) at His Second Coming and destroy *all* remaining elements of the governments of man — all at one time. Then the kingdom of Jesus the Messiah will fill the whole earth, and the knowledge of God will wash over the earth like an ocean.

This is the great promise of Daniel's statue: A unified kingdom in which every Christian has citizenship. At present, we are only ambassadors in the kingdoms of today. But as ambassadors we are empowered to appeal on behalf of Jesus to all citizens, of all kingdoms. It is an awesome privilege and responsibility.

# Before the End

## Daniel — A Prophetic Life

Now that you have examined the prophecies of Daniel that have been unsealed, I'm sure you've been amazed. But before we close our study, we're going to explore the life of Daniel the prophet because, quite frankly, it also was amazing.

The book of Daniel contains many key prophecies about the time before the return of Jesus. Interspersed among these prophetic visions are stories about the life of Daniel and his three friends, Shadrach, Meshach, and Abednego. If we look at these stories closely, it becomes apparent that they act as parables, teaching us spiritual life-lessons. Looking at them even more closely, we notice that each one of the stories represents an Old Testament type and a foreshadowing of what is to come during the end times. I find it immensely interesting that the prophet who gave us some of the most detailed information about the time before Jesus's return lived a life that foreshadowed some of the very events he prophesied about!

**The Captivity**

The book of Daniel begins with King Nebuchadnezzar of Babylon besieging Jerusalem and ransacking the Holy items from the Temple of God. He then carries into captivity some of the youth of Israel, including Daniel and his friends, where they are required to serve the King in his court. Interestingly, this is exactly how the Great Tribulation begins, as well. Luke records Jesus's words about this time:

> *But when you see Jerusalem surrounded by armies, then recognize that her desolation is near. Then those who are in Judea must flee to the mountains, and those who are in the midst of the city must leave, and those who are in the country must not enter the city; because these are days of vengeance, so that all things which are written will be fulfilled. Woe to those who are pregnant and to those who are nursing babies in those days; for there will be great distress upon the land and wrath to this people; and they will fall by the edge of the sword, and will be led captive into all the nations; and Jerusalem will be trampled under-foot by the Gentiles until the times of the Gentiles are fulfilled.* **(Luke 21: 20-24)**

This passage was foreshadowed in Daniel's day and again in AD 70 when the Romans destroyed the city and the Temple. But the final fulfillment occurs in the future, when, as Jesus tells us, *all things* which are written will be fulfilled. Until then, *all things* will *not* be fulfilled. These things must wait for the return of Jesus.

## The Mark of The Beast

Daniel and his friends were taken captive to serve King Nebuchadnezzar in his court. One of the requirements of their new life was that they eat the same food that the King ate, which included meat sacrificed to the King's idols. Daniel and his friends requested that they be allowed to subsist on a diet of vegetables instead. Ashpenaz, Chief of the Eunuchs, who was in charge of the young men, was skeptical at first. But Daniel wisely requested a 10-day test of the vegan diet. Miraculously, after the test period, Daniel and his friends were healthier than the other captives.

We know that during the Great Tribulation, the false prophet will enforce the mark of the Beast. No one will be able to buy or sell without the mark. Not taking the mark may be considered a form of *physical suicide*: In a culture such as ours in which obtaining food, water and shelter depends entirely on buying and selling, not taking the mark will effectively make these things impossible to obtain.

Unfortunately, taking the mark of the Beast is *spiritual suicide*. God's Word states:

> *Then another angel, a third one, followed them, saying with a loud voice, "If anyone worships the Beast and his image, and receives a mark on his forehead or on his hand, he also will drink of the wine of the wrath of God, which is mixed in full strength in the cup of His anger; and he will be tormented with fire and brimstone in the presence of the holy angels and in the presence of the Lamb. And the smoke of their torment goes up forever and ever; they have no rest day and night, those who worship the Beast and his image, and whoever receives the mark of his name." Here is the perseverance of the saints who keep the commandments of God and their faith in Jesus.* **(Rev 14: 9-12)**

This is incredibly clear. Anyone who takes the mark of the Beast experiences the wrath of God. This will place all believers in a difficult position. But just like Daniel, we must refuse the king's food (the Antichrist's food). We must not take the mark. And just like Daniel, we must have faith that God will provide for us. In Rev 12, God shows one means by which He will provide for some of his people:

> *Then the woman fled into the wilderness where she has a place prepared by God, so that there she would be nourished for one thousand two hundred and sixty days.* **(Rev 12:6)**

Notice that He (God) provides nourishment for the woman for the 1,260 days. There are many other references to God's faithfulness during times of need. In Daniel, He shows how He can maintain us, even with what, at the time, may have seemed like an inadequate diet.

## The Abomination of Desolation

In Dan 2, we find the story of Nebuchadnezzar's dream of a huge metal statue. God helped Daniel interpret the dream, and Daniel informed Nebuchadnezzar that Babylon was the head of gold on the statue and that other kingdoms would assume pre-eminence after Babylon fell.

Nebuchadnezzar obviously didn't like what God revealed to him in his dream. He didn't want Babylon's kingdom to end, and he made his own statue in defiance of God's revealed Word. The statue Nebuchadnezzar created was made entirely of gold – the metal representing Babylon – rather than multiple metals. He was in essence saying to God, "You may have a statue of different metals and think other kingdoms will replace Babylon, but my statue is only gold. Babylon will last forever!"

In Dan 3 we learn more about this statue:

> *Nebuchadnezzar the king made an image of gold, the height of which was sixty cubits and its width six cubits; he set it up on the plain of Dura in the province of Babylon.* **(Dan 3:1)**

This statue is definitely a foreshadowing of the Abomination. First, it's a statue of gold and therefore represents the kingdom of Babylon. Second, we know from Rev 13 that the final Abomination will be an image of the fourth Beast Empire. And third, we see the numbers 60 and six in the above passage. The number of the final Beast Empire will be 600, 60, and six *(666)*. God's Word is telling us that *this image* is like the final one that is to come!

After the image was set up, Nebuchadnezzar commanded everyone to bow to the image. In the Septuagint Old Testament, the Greek word for *bow down* is *proskuneó*, which is the identical Greek word translated in Revelation as *worship* in this passage about the Abomination of Desolation:

> *And it was given to him to give breath to the image of the Beast, so that the image of the Beast would even speak and cause as many as do not worship the image of the Beast to be killed.* **(Rev 13:15)**

This Greek word literally means *to kiss the ground in reverence to something greater*. This is a perfect picture of how *Muslims bow to Mecca*.

We also see in Dan 3 that Nebuchadnezzar ordered a call to worship to be played by an orchestra of instruments. It was upon that signal that the bowing was to take place. This is also a perfect picture of the *Muslim call to prayer* that plays from their minarets prior to each of these prayer sessions, during which they *kiss the ground*.

## Persecution

Finally, in Dan 6 we encounter the most famous episode in Daniel's life, the night he spent in the lion's den. What does the lion's den represent? Who is the lion? Peter tells us:

> *Be of sober spirit, be on the alert. Your adversary, the devil, prowls around like a roaring Lion, seeking someone to devour.* **(1 Pet 5: 8)**

Why is Daniel thrown to the lions? Because he prayed to Yehovah when prayer to the true God was made illegal, and because he was betrayed by his associates. During the end times believers must also plan for a time when the worship of God will be illegal and they will be betrayed by former brothers and sisters in Christ who have fallen away. Jesus himself tells us:

> *Then they will deliver you to tribulation, and will kill you, and you will be hated by all nations because of My name. At that time many will fall away and will betray one another and hate one another.* **(Matt 24: 9-10 )**

Daniel's night in the lion's den not only reveals whose den believers will be thrown into (Satan's), it also reveals their possible deliverance. The angel of God shut the mouths of the hungry lions. But notice that Daniel was *saved in the midst of the trial, not from the trial*. This also is a picture of what believers need to plan for. God will save them in their trial.

> *No temptation has overtaken you but such as is common to man; and God is faithful, who will not allow you to be tempted beyond what you are able, but with the*

*temptation will provide the way of escape also, so that you will be able to endure it.* **(1 Cor 10:13)**

Notice that the escape is *not* that believers are *removed* from the trial, but that they are enabled to *endure* the trial. In this way, our faith is increased.

These foreshadowings of the Tribulation in Daniel's life are not coincidence. God has given them to us in the same book of the Bible in which many of the original prophecies occur in order to deepen our understanding of the Great Tribulation, so that we might prepare!

As we continue to contemplate the prophecies of Daniel which have now been unsealed, let's keep in mind his prophetic life. It was one that foreshadowed much of what he would later have revealed to him. He was a *doer* of the Word, living in action exactly what he preached.

# The End

## In the Lion's Den

Daniel served the Lord in exile. His was not an easy life, working as he did in the courts of foreign, pagan kings. As we discussed in the previous article, his life was a foreshadowing of what many will endure in the end times.

From Daniel's perspective, most of us — at least those of us in Western nations — have lived an easy life. But if the book of Daniel is now unsealed, as we believe, that may soon change. Because *the end times have begun*. Although those who encounter future tribulation during this period may not face *actual* lions, as Daniel did, we will be in the den of a Beast much more fearsome, one that devours not just the body, but the soul, as well. That Beast — and those who serve him — are in our future as we enter the end times.

That is the *take-away* from this book. And yet, even though we face great peril and uncertainty in the end times, God has provided us with a road map of sorts, to help us find our way. He did this through the prophecies of Daniel. Using Daniel's visions, we can know with certainty that God has ordained and sanctioned both the process and the players of these difficult times. And we can be just as certain that if we take the time to *understand* these things, then the events of these times will reveal themselves just as God has planned. That is, after all, the purpose of prophecy — to help us foresee, prepare for, and overcome the events that God has ordained by His Sovereign Will. In order to do that, however, we must be students of His Word.

Within the pages of this book, we have attempted to articulate our understanding of what the now-unsealed words of God are communicating in the prophecies of Daniel. This is a Holy obligation, a sacred trust. A lot is at stake: Lives and souls may depend on proper interpretation of these prophecies. And though we have labored and studied much in the pursuit of the truth of these matters, we are certainly not infallible; only God is.

With that in mind, we suggest that you carefully study our work, with this book in one hand and your Bible in the other. We trust that you will find the book to be a valuable guide. But the Bible is your rock, your foundation, and your ultimate source of truth. The Holy Spirit is your only true teacher.

We would like to leave you with the following key points from the many details discussed in this book. We ask you to consider these carefully as you make preparations to enter the Lion's Den.

1. In Article Two, we discussed in detail why we believe that the *legs of iron* of Nebuchadnezzar's statue are the *Islamic Caliphate* and not Rome. This is a *key understanding*. The vast majority of Western Christians are looking to Europe and the papacy to be the source from which the coming evil arises. If this popular view is mistaken, the eyes of the Church will be in the wrong place and considering the wrong events as the end times progress.

2. In Article Three, we established that the Beast is a supernatural combination of three aspects: He is simultaneously man, kingdom, and demon.

Christians need to recognize and understand the complexity of this evil that will exist during the end times. It is this *hidden, other-worldly, and demonic* aspect that will cause many to underestimate the Man of Sin. In the flesh, nations and churches will not be his equal; and, as scripture says, the saints will be given into his hands for much of *time, times, and half a time*. Be strong in your faith, because we know how the story ends. The Lord will destroy the Antichrist with nothing more than the breath from His Holy mouth.

3. In Article Four, we discussed what may be one of the *most significant findings* in this book: The fact that the events of Dan 8 remain *in the future*. If this is a proper understanding, as we believe it to be, then nearly everything that the Church believes about Daniel will change. *First*, it means that the end times have already begun and that, by extension, the book of Daniel is now unsealed. *Second*, it means that a significant war between Iran and a Turkish-based coalition looms in the near future. And *third*, we discussed that a principal role of the Church in an end times world will be as *Apocalyptic Evangelists*. God wants us to be doers of the Word, especially when all seems lost and so many souls are at risk.

4. In Article Five, we established which events will precede the 70th Week of Daniel. Regardless which rapture theory you presently trust, these are events that we can rather safely predict will occur prior to *any* rapture. We also discussed in detail the

geography of the Antichrist's early career, including the likely area from which he will arise — which will be the Middle East, not Europe.

5. Articles Six, Seven, Eight, and Ten all provide unique details and a look at *history in advance* as we anticipate the Antichrist's blood-thirsty career through the prophecies of Daniel. We trust you will take these prognostications seriously, because understanding them will help you prepare for — and minister during — the deadly reign of the Antichrist.

6. In Article Nine, we reveal that Satan took great pains to prevent Daniel from receiving the interpretation of prophecy in Dan 10-12, which depict both the rise and fall of Little Horn and the eventual rescue of all who are written in the Book of Life.

7. In Article Eleven, we offer suggestions regarding the relationship between the Jewish Feasts of the Lord (Lev 23) and the timing of *time, times, and half a time*.

8. In Article Twelve, we propose a possible link between the workings of the Antichrist and the United Nations; and we offer several scenarios for how this organization might figure into end times events.

Finally, we humbly acknowledge that not everything we have concluded in these pages may be entirely correct. That said, we firmly believe that *scripture interprets scripture*, and, wherever possible, our conclusions are based upon the truth of what God has revealed in His Holy Word. In our opinion, every prior commentary on Daniel has fallen well short of this truth, due in large part to God's long-term sealing of the prophecies. Because the vast majority of this book represents *newly-revealed understanding*, we believe it is worthy of careful, Spirit-led study.

If you have questions and wish to contact us, or if you wish to follow our ministry, please use the email address and website information included in the introductory pages. If you are interested in following-up on this study, our recent book, *How to Prepare for the Last Days* (2019), is probably the most detailed book available on getting ready for the return of Jesus.

Even though we don't know you personally, we have prayed for each of our Lord's disciples who read this book. May He bless you with his presence and guide you as you study His truth.

Nelson and Bob

Made in the USA
Las Vegas, NV
04 May 2024